Bulletin Boards and 3-D Showcases That Capture Them with Pizzazz

Bulletin Boards and 3-D Showcases That Capture Them with Pizzazz

Karen Hawthorne

and

Jane E. Gibson

Illustrated by Jane E. Gibson

1999
LIBRARIES UNLIMITED, INC.
and Its Division
Teacher Ideas Press
Englewood, Colorado

LIBRARIES UNLIMITED, INC.
and Its Division
Teacher Ideas Press
P.O. Box 6633
Englewood, CO 80155-6633
1-800-237-6124
www.lu.com

Library of Congress Cataloging-in-Publication Data

Hawthorne, Karen.
    Bulletin boards and 3-D showcases that capture them with pizzazz /
Karen Hawthorne and Jane E. Gibson ; illustrated by Jane E. Gibson.
    ix, 145 p. 22x28 cm.
    Includes index.
    ISBN 1-56308-695-6 (softbound)
    1. Bulletin boards.   I. Gibson, Jane E.   II. Title.
LB1043.58.H38   1999
373. 133'56--dc21   99-11163
                                                        CIP

Contents

Acknowledgments

We would like to extend our deepest thanks to our editor, Betty Morris, at Libraries Unlimited who gave us very valuable information about the principles of design that are incorporated into Chapter One. She has also been very helpful throughout the process of creating this book.

We would also like to thank Cheryl Eckl, our Author Relations Coordinator, who answered our many questions and calmed our worries that we would do the technical processes right.

Sincerely,

Karen Hawthorne and *Jane E. Gibson*

Introduction

The main objective of bulletin boards and showcase displays should be to capture the attention of students. This is especially a challenge in secondary schools. This challenge is often met by using a multidimensional approach in the presentation. The ideas in this book are designed to attract students in junior and senior high school but can easily be adapted to any grade, subject, and budget.

Bulletin boards are the keys to student input, conversation, excitement, and motivation about reading. An eye-catching, thought-provoking bulletin board may be the beginning of a student becoming a lifelong reader and user of the library. This is especially true of the secondary students who sometimes picture themselves as too "cool" to show enthusiasm about reading.

The bulletin boards featured in this book have been the favorites of students in grades 7–12. Adding a real object (rake, shoes, stuffed animal) seems to attract much more comment and positive responses than the plain, flat displays that are so often used. These bulletin boards speak to the students, and the students respond by saying, "I like that board!"; "Where's that book?"; or even just, "Cool idea."

It is the intention of the authors to facilitate the media specialist's and teacher's jobs when they ponder, "What am I going to put on the bulletin board or showcase this month?"

All bulletin boards and showcases featured in this book have been created by the authors. The designs for the bulletin boards and showcases are presented on two facing pages in this book, with bulletin boards on the left and showcases on the right. This format, using facing pages, provides different ideas for using the same theme either as a flat display or as a three-dimensional display. Any resemblance to any design or pictures from any other source is purely coincidental.

Chapter One — Getting Started

Bulletin boards come in all shapes and sizes. The most common one, of course, is the typical rectangle shape. However, bulletin boards are not limited to traditional shapes. Bulletin boards may be created using hallways, ceilings, walls, floors, alcoves, doors, windows, corners, and even staircases. A complete wall can become a giant bulletin board that excites and captures the mind of the student or patron. There really are no boundaries for bulletin boards or one's imagination. These display areas may go from ceiling to floor or off each side of the board. Never, ever, let the lack of a bulletin board attached to the wall prevent the creation of exciting and thought-provoking displays. There is no excuse for no bulletin boards. Be creative!

Bulletin boards and showcases are not a luxury. They are necessities. It is a proven fact that students are motivated by visual displays. Students do not always comment about the showcases and boards, but when they do comment they prove the belief that a showcase or bulletin board is worth a hundred words. Seniors have commented about showcases and bulletin boards used in their seventh grade year when they check out of the library upon graduation. Experts report that students learn 10 percent by listening and 80 percent by viewing. Students also remember 20 percent of what they hear and 50 percent of what they see and hear. These statistics and comments reinforce the crucial need for bulletin boards and displays. They also explain why students do notice and remember these eye-catching efforts.

This chapter includes hints, suggestions, and guidelines that may be followed. These ideas are merely possibilities to improve the showcases, displays, and bulletin boards found in the library and classrooms. However, the bulletin boards featured in this book do not always follow these suggestions. Experiment with these ideas and decide which ones work best for the situations and localities being considered.

PRINCIPLES OF DESIGN

Balance, movement, unity, and simplicity are the four basic principles of design. *Balance* is an important principle to follow. Balance of the bulletin board or project is achieved by the positioning of the elements that have been selected. There are two basic types of balance: formal and informal.

Formal balance uses a symmetrical design and conveys parallel messages. The formal design is divided equally. The props and images project identical reflections if the board is cut in half. These components are usually centered on the board or in the showcase. Most of the boards and showcases in this book employ informal design; however, a striking, simplistic message may be conveyed using a formally designed board.

Informal balance utilizes a more flexible design. Suggestions to remember in informal balance are:

1. Two or more small shapes balance a larger one.

2. A small shape placed low balances a larger one placed high.

3. A brightly colored small shape balances a dull, large shape.

4. A small, interesting, or unusual shape balances a large, ordinary one.

Movement is another design principle, and it should flow toward the center of interest. The logical eye path of the observer should be considered when planning the bulletin board's movement. In the Western world, eye movement is trained to move from left to right and from top to bottom. The eye also is trained to move in a circular motion clockwise. When planning the design, mentally divide the bulletin board into four equal quadrants. The typical eye path starts in the upper left quadrant and retains 41 percent of the initial fixation to the left and above center. Then the eye movement tracks 20 percent into the right upper quadrant and moves downward to the right lower quadrant, where it views only 14 percent. It then continues clockwise into the lower left quadrant, where 25 percent is viewed. The observer's eye initially sees the upper left corner and focuses on the center of interest. The bulletin board artist controls this desired eye movement by using various techniques. String, yarn, ribbon, and other media may be tacked or pinned to the board in a manner that leads the eye to see the whole board arrangement. A good arrangement displays the visual elements in a pattern that captivates the viewer's attention and directs it toward the important details. An imbalance of the board that results in a disproportionate weight distribution of items tends to be psychologically disturbing. Many times, it is very obvious to the trained eye that the board is not balanced. Often this imbalance can be used to an advantage by catching the passing student's fancy. Follow your instincts.

Unity, the third principle of design, is achieved with a sense of cohesion that is reached by the use of space. Unity occurs when the board "clicks" or becomes complete. This completeness may be reached by providing blank space around the visuals and avoiding blank spaces within the visuals that divide it into separate compositions. The usual rule of thumb is less is best. Leave enough space to make the elements grab the viewer's attention.

Simplicity is an important design principle. Limit the number of topics in a visual. Only have one idea at a time. The most common theme of the boards in this book is READ. Many times that four letter word is the only slogan. It is so simple, but it gets to the heart and purpose of the library. The key is to display something unique that will inspire the student to READ books about the theme of the board or to research that theme.

TOOLS OF DESIGN

There are seven tools of design: space, shape, texture, size, line, arrangement, and color. These tools are all valuable, and an outstanding board is not achieved unless they are implemented.

Space as defined in this section deals with blank space. Space sets objects apart and influences the value, importance, and stability of the visual. The individual elements are emphasized through the use of blank space. Practice with this tool until the comfort zone is reached. Add items, then stand back, take some off and add more to it. Repeat this procedure until the results are pleasing. Trust your intuition.

Shape employs the use of two- and three-dimensional objects. Collect and use a kaleidoscope of shapes and materials, such as corrugated cardboard, Styrofoam, various fabrics, metallic papers such as aluminum foil, shadow boxes, models, and sculptures. Squares, circles, triangles, oblongs, and rectangles add interesting designs to the board and ignite the viewer's interest and imagination. Shape keeps the board from becoming boring or routine.

Texture is an important tool of design. Shoes, feathers, fur, crayons, yarns, mirrors, silk and plastic flowers, gloves, Styrofoam balls, strings, ropes, models, baseball bats, toys, dolls, golf clubs, racquets, and myriad other objects should be used to attract the student's or patron's interest. These items give the boards texture, and many, of course, get touched and patted. Students love to see real items on the boards and in the showcases. The use of old toys that were once old friends of the students bring back nostalgic memories that halt traffic by the boards. These recycled toys and objects send the students' minds scurrying down memory lane and reinforce the love of reading.

Size is another significant tool of design. Use different sizes of visuals to draw attention to the board. Balance the size of the visual with the lettering. A general rule is to make the lettering 1/25 the height of the visual. However, many times, the slogan or caption is what is being emphasized and the visual is smaller. Experiment with size to achieve the effect that attracts the most attention and best conveys the desired theme.

Line is used in design to direct the attention of the viewer. It is also used to accent the slogan or visual by highlighting it. Examples of line usage would be an arrow as a pointer, a string design pulling the eye toward the desired object of attention, or a simple border drawing attention to one segment of the board.

Arrangement is one of the most versatile tools of design. The placement of visuals to attract attention and to focus on the topic is very important. The arrangement directs the attention to key details. Pin the visuals one way; step back and view the overall effect. Then pin the visuals another way and inspect that arrangement. Many times the arrangement that feels right is the one that should be used. Never forget to experiment with different and unique arrangements.

Color is the most powerful tool of design. Color creates the mood of the board. Excitement is created when red, yellow, or orange is used. A serene mood is created by the use of gray, green, or blue as the dominant color. A mood of peace and contentment is imparted by using blue. Moods of power and vitality are evoked when red is used. To stress strength, reliability, and honesty, use green and red. A mood of security and self-esteem is created when green and blue are used together. There are old rules concerning the use of color, but in today's colorful world, anything goes. However, psychologists still agree that colors do emit certain vibes. Generally accepted interpretations are:

> Pinks signify femininity.
>
> Blues signify masculinity.
>
> Browns denote earth tones.
>
> Browns, blacks, whites, and grays are neutral.
>
> Gold is commonly used to highlight dark colors.
>
> Silver is commonly used to highlight light and pastel colors.
>
> Cool colors are blue, green, and violet.
>
> Hot colors are the reds and oranges, and they also signify fire.
>
> Yellow is a warm, bright, happy color and also signifies caution.
>
> Red signifies stop.
>
> Green signifies go.
>
> Blue signifies truth.
>
> Purple signifies royalty.
>
> White signifies purity.

Colors that complement each other are blue/orange; yellow/violet; and red/green. Split complements are red/yellow green/blue green; yellow/red violet/blue violet; and blue/yellow orange/red orange. Three color schemes that are visually appealing are orange/green/violet and red/yellow/blue.

Analogous colors are three colors side by side on the color wheel. They add attractiveness to the bulletin board and displays. These analogous groups are yellow green/green/blue green; violet/blue violet/red violet; yellow/yellow green/green; blue/blue green/blue violet; blue/blue violet/violet; red/red violet/red orange; orange/red orange/yellow orange; and yellow/yellow orange/yellow green. Use these groups to blend and impart soothing effects on the viewer.

The use of color influences the way the viewer sees the board. The board appears to recede from the observer when cool colors are used. When warm colors are used the board appears to approach the observer. Important cues and slogans in the visual should be highlighted in red and orange to enable the message to leap toward the viewer.

Contrasting colors are used to emphasize points, create mood, provide visual interest, and improve legibility. Monochromatic boards that use only black, white, and grays are quite striking if emphasized with a touch of bright color such as red and blue or blue and yellow. Use contrasting colors for letters and backgrounds to make the board more legible. Green on white; black on yellow; black on white; red on yellow; red on white; and white on black are contrasting colors that increase readability and visibility.

A collection of differently colored backgrounds is essential for the beginning librarian or teacher. Cut the exact size background for your boards and laminate it for repeated use. Basic colors and suggested uses are:

Black—Halloween, Science Fiction, Night Scenes, Space
Brown—Fall, Back to School, Fall Sports
Red—Winter Holidays, St. Valentine's Day, School Colors
Orange—Halloween, Spring, Fall
Yellow—Spring, Summer
Blue—Outdoor Sky, Snow Scenes, Winter, Spring Sky
Green—Spring, St. Patrick's Day, Christmas
White—Snow, Winter

The top or bottom half of any background can be covered with generic meadows, falling leaves, snow banks, and innumerable ground or sky covers. Be creative with color. Use of the color wheel is a definite asset if contrasts and complements are desired. (See Fig. 1.1.)

Fig 1.1. Color Wheel.

The positive applications of color are many. Color enhances and enriches any bulletin board. Mood influences, emotional responses, and movement indication is achieved by the use and selection of color. Depicting actual colors of the images chosen heightens their realism. Color use points out the similarities and differences of these images. The important information or theme of the board is highlighted by the use of color.

The next step in bulletin board construction is applying the guidelines and suggestions that have been discussed. Remember the basic bulletin board tips that are recommended to incorporate every time:

1. Plan arrangement carefully. Items should be balanced attractively. Slogans should be catchy and grab the viewer's attention.

2. Pin the arrangement before final fastening or stapling. It is easier to rearrange.

3. Change bulletin boards at least once a month; more often is even better.

4. Add real items to add texture, to prevent boredom, and to capture the students' attention.

5. Keep it simple. Less is better. Too much can take away from the desired overall effect.

6. Eye appeal is important. Color is an important factor in catching attention. Black and white can be very dramatic. Use of analogous color schemes on the color wheel can be very eye appealing; however, students today use wild colors together.

7. Be current on student interests. Use your observations of their dress, reading interests, movies, and what they are currently studying. They like to know that the teacher or librarian cares enough to notice. Featuring the summer's blockbuster movie (usually a book) in a back-to-school board or showcase lets the students know that the library is up to date on current trends.

BACKGROUND

Backgrounds are very influential on the overall effect. They "ground" the display and set the basic mood being conveyed. Materials to be used for backgrounds may be as varied as one's imagination. Typical backgrounds are usually constructed from paper, plastic garbage bags, vinyl, and fabric. Remember the aspects of color and texture choices when choosing the background.

Paper of all descriptions may be used. Craft paper, butcher paper, art paper, construction paper, brown paper sacks, wrapping paper (one of the best choices because of the unlimited scenes and styles), aluminum foil, wallpaper, newspapers, and even sandpaper may be used. The first time that new paper is used for a background, take time to measure the bulletin board and cut the paper to size. This extra time and effort will pay off in future time saved as the background is used again and again. Laminate the backgrounds, if possible, so that they may be reused for years. Do not let the width of the laminator limit making these backgrounds reusable.

Just fold the paper in half, cut along the fold, laminate it, then reassemble it on the display. Watch for marked-down wrapping paper or wallpaper patterns that may be useful for backgrounds. Fish, rain forests, stars, and a multitude of themes for backgrounds are available for thrifty prices for the perpetual bulletin board shopper. Many cities have specialty shopping outlets where discontinued patterns are sold daily for at least 50 percent off. Capitalize on the savings found at these outlets.

The use of fabric is unlimited for backgrounds and brings even more unique textures to the board. Bandanna prints; flags; red, white, and blue prints; red and green burlap; velvets; silks; corduroy; and many other fabric scraps found at home or in stores are easily stapled to the bulletin boards for interesting backgrounds and extra texture. One of the most versatile fabric backgrounds used in the showcases in this book is a pastel upholstery piece that has been used to portray gorgeous sunrises and sunsets for beach scenes and Australian and Hawaiian features. Its flexibility has been worth the sale price paid for it 10 years ago. It is used at least once a year.

BORDERS

Borders are an added attraction to showcases and bulletin boards. One must decide whether a border is necessary. If a jungle or outdoor scene is being constructed, then a border might not add anything to it and could in fact detract from its realism. Many of the boards featured in this book were used without a border. If the background material has been cut precisely, then a border may not be necessary. Many times a border is used to cover staples, pins, or raggedy corners. Other objects such as leaves, stars, miniature books, or flowers may be strategically placed to cover staples. Often a border makes the board perfect. The fake fur Scottie dog bulletin board featured in this book is an example of the border offering the perfect finishing touch. Finding a border with black and white Scotties with bows completed the unique statement this board makes. Borders come from numerous sources. They may be purchased from local teacher supply stores, mail orders, or cut out if student aides or extra time are available. Purchased borders include patterns and solids. Many of the patterned borders look like photographs and add realistic graphics to the board. Solid borders can be quite striking depending upon color choices. Often a border suggests an idea for an entire layout.

Nontraditional borders are created by various applications. Using a leafy vine draped across the top of the board evokes a forest or garden scene. Cotton batting turns the bottom border into a field of snow. Green burlap creates the illusion of grass. Be creative and imaginative with the unlimited possibilities that are available for borders.

Die-cut patterns (such as a leaf, snowflake or jack-o'-lantern) may be taped together in the exact measurements of the board and then laminated for reuse. These borders create a striking board, especially if that same die cut pattern is enlarged on the opaque or overhead projector. The enlarged pattern then becomes the center of a completely coordinated board. The result is one of simplicity and often turns into one of the most striking and successful boards created.

LETTERS

Letters are one of the most essential elements of a board or showcase. They can be time-consuming and tedious, but hopefully, the following tips will simplify this chore. Heavy precut letters in a variety of colors and patterns are available for purchase from teacher supply stores or catalogs. These are relatively inexpensive. Begin a basic supply of letters by starting with large and small letters in black, white, and red. Then add other colors and patterns when the budget permits. Many of these packets are coordinated with a matching border. The problem that many librarians and teachers run into with patterned letters is that they are not as versatile as the solids, or often the patterns clash with other backgrounds. These patterned letters work best on a solid background. Use good judgment when making these purchases. A new librarian or teacher just starting out in a career would be wise to purchase these basic colors and laminate them, if possible, to protect this investment.

Purchased pin back letters of 1 inch, 1½ inches, 2 inches, 2½ inches, and 3 inches sizes are available in black, white, and red. Begin purchases with the tall white size and add the others as budgets allow. These letters are available from library supply catalogs and local teacher supply stores. One set purchased 30 years ago is still going strong. Its purchase has been well worth the initial investment, even on a beginning teacher's salary. The time and effort that has been saved by using these letters cannot be stressed enough.

A letter-cutting machine, if available, is a blessing. Use it to cut out letters from construction paper, wrapping paper, card stock, and almost any type of paper that is not too thick. Laminate the paper before cutting for permanence and efficient time management. The time that this machine saves for teachers and librarians is miraculous.

Computer-generated letters give the flexibility of being able to choose unique and numerous fonts and styles (bold, outline, shadow) that complement the theme. First, print the slogan. Then enlarge it with a copier or opaque projector, depending upon the size desired. Color and laminate it for permanence. This type of lettering can be the most time-consuming, but if the budget or school setting does not have the other options available, this method is superior to freehanding letters or tracing around stencils and cutting them out by hand. The use of colored paper when enlarging slogans and themes also adds dramatic color to the board. The introduction of the computer into print shops and art departments has improved life for the teacher and librarian.

LEAVES AND FLOWERS

Leaves and flowers add new dimensions and textures to the bulletin boards and showcases featured in this book. A good source of artificial leaves and flowers is garage sales. Buy those sad, dusty flower arrangements and fake plants, then dismantle them. Swish silk flowers around in a sink full of warm, sudsy water. Gently shake and hang them upside down to dry, and they are rejuvenated and ready to enhance the boards and showcases. Plastic flowers are also easily washed and dried.

Leaves, especially in autumn colors, may be purchased in the hobby section of large discount stores at a very low cost. Plan ahead for next year and buy them in the postseason markdown sales. It is cost-effective to purchase a leafy "vine," which can be used in a multitude of ways. The vine may become a hanging vine for stuffed animals to hang out on in the showcase or it can be wrapped around the rope of a swing on the bulletin board. These leaves and flowers are added attractions and bring the board or showcase to life. They are especially helpful in plugging holes, covering staples, or balancing the overall effect. There are hundreds of ways that vines and garlands add texture and dimension to these creations. The letter-cutting machine is another resource for leaves and flowers. Many schools have dies for leaves, flowers, and shapes other than letters.

OPAQUE PROJECTOR

The opaque projector is a valuable tool to help the bulletin board artist. Use the opaque projector to save money and create hard-to-find items. Its use cannot be emphasized enough. Anything that can be found in a picture can be turned into a reproduction for the displays. Items made on the opaque projector are usually flat, so this technique is extremely helpful in creating backgrounds. The opaque projector is also used on fabrics such as fake fur, vinyl, or prints to create creatures and friends for the showcase or board. These items may be produced by implementing the following steps: Use masking tape to fasten a background of poster board, fabric, or other materials to a wall, or staple it directly onto the board. Project the desired picture or design onto the background material; then trace the shape right onto the background. Cut out and laminate. Experiment with different techniques. The overhead projector works in the same manner, but the image must first be transformed into a transparency. Enlarge an image, such as the school emblem or a design desired for use on a piece of poster board, then color it and cut it out. Adding a scrap piece of wood or Styrofoam by gluing it to the back of the image results in a multidimensional board instead of a flat one. Students always notice the school mascots, and this instills school pride; they are especially observant if the mascot is reading.

MISCELLANEOUS PROPS

There are numerous miscellaneous props that enhance bulletin boards and showcases. Many items on the basic supplies list are already available at the school library or at home. Garage sales, postholiday sales, and spring-cleaning yield exciting props, ideas, and decorations. Twigs and branches from the yard, unclaimed scarves and mittens from the lost-and-found, colorful pictures from donated magazines, and children's old toys spark an idea for a creative, eye-catching bulletin board. The recycling of kids' toys or toys from garage sales cannot be emphasized enough. These toys capture many of the most reluctant readers; invariably, they are overheard saying, "I had one of those, but my mom threw it out." The memories of the fun experienced with these toys transfers to the fun of the play on words that might inspire them to read a book from the featured genre or theme. One major rule that cannot be stressed enough is always keep your eyes and mind open to the unlimited ideas from which bulletin boards can be created.

STORAGE

After the librarian or teacher starts collecting treasures and props for the bulletin board, a big problem arises. How are these fabulous discoveries and creations going to be kept for future use? Empty computer and duplicating paper boxes are excellent storage compartments for bulletin board supplies. They are a convenient size for easy handling and storage in almost any facility. Since some supplies and props are used in many different displays, trying to keep a box for each board theme is not the most efficient method. Experience has proven that it is better to store like components together in labeled boxes; for example, all leaves in one box, letters in another, background fabrics in yet another. The generic items such as leaves, seashells, trees, and cotton batting found on the supply list should be labeled and stacked alphabetically to facilitate locating and speedily changing the boards monthly.

The boxes can be neatly stacked upon each other, stored on shelves or under work tables. Label them plainly on both ends with a permanent marker. If there is too much writing on the ends of the boxes, paint over it with a craft paint or tape a clean piece of paper onto the ends of the box (the painting option would be more permanent). Then label the boxes. Drawers in a map case are perfect for storing posters, slogans, and large pictures. There are various oversized storage cartons available for purchase. Look through supply catalogs for other ideas on storage, but a map case works best of all. A file cabinet can also be used to store letters and slogans. Use the length of the drawers to make lateral files by cutting cardboard in the appropriate lengths to divide the drawers into sections. These pieces of cardboard can be labeled with the slogans and makes finding them much easier. Slogans and words that have been laminated in strips may be stored in this manner.

Background papers may be rolled loosely, held with a rubber band, and stored in large trash cans. A smaller can may be used for shorter rolls. The rolls may be labeled by small writing on the reverse side of a corner of the paper or by inserting a label under the rubber band holding the rolls.

Chapter Two

Putting It Together

Developing the display is the next step in becoming a master of bulletin board and showcase creations. Generally, there are months and holidays for which ideas are easily generated. Other times, it is very difficult even to begin thinking about what to do that month. Historically, back-to-school time seems to be a difficult time to decide what to feature. Students have been having a good time working or doing summertime activities, and they are not necessarily thinking about getting back to reading and researching. This lack of interest is normal and challenges the bulletin board artist to entice them back into the library. On the one hand, January always seems to be another time that is difficult to decide what to create; these problem months require even more effort to create unusual and innovative displays. On the other hand, fall seems to be an easy season for generating slogans for theme boards and showcases. Scarecrows, autumn leaves, ornamental corn, and hay bales are quickly assembled to carry out these seasonal ideas. Back up the autumn showcase or bookcase display with fall bulletin boards and displays throughout the area. Sports themes work well during their respective seasons; posters of sports figures can be used to promote almost any subject.

Another consideration in developing holiday displays is local community preferences and its views on the subject of holiday observances in the schools. Most public schools allow holiday displays involving Halloween, Thanksgiving, and some variation of the December holidays: Hanukkah, Christmas, and other multicultural celebrations. If local opinion prefers, October can be represented with a football, softball, or soccer theme instead of Halloween. Santa Claus is generally accepted for the Yule season. In private schools, or where allowed, religious holidays offer opportunities to display wonderful collections of crèches, menorahs, and dreidels borrowed from faculty and staff. Thanksgiving can be represented historically (pilgrims), mathematically (how many quarter-pound servings from a 21-pound turkey?), or, as shown in this book, to emphasize reading ("Give Thanks for Books"). St. Valentine's Day does not have to be limited to heart cutouts. A display of "Heartbreakers and Tearjerkers" or the familiar "Books We All Love" can highlight romance novels or classic favorites. Local opinion and preferences often suggest appropriate ways to handle the development of displays.

The librarian or teacher should develop a bulletin board or showcase by implementing the following guidelines:

1. Decide upon an objective.

2. Generate a theme.

3. Incorporate the theme into a slogan.

4. Work out a rough layout.

5. Gather the materials.

6. Put up the display.

OBJECTIVE

Deciding upon the objective is sometimes the hardest step in getting started. The most often asked question after a showcase or board is put up is, "Where do you get your ideas?" or "Do you have a book of ideas?" or "How do you come up with these great ideas?" Almost every faculty member says, "You ought to write a book to help us out!" They seem to have no trouble imagining these ideas transformed into their subject content.

Basically, ideas are collected from everywhere if teachers and librarians train themselves to look for opportunities to turn anything into a way to promote reading, books, and the various curriculum areas. The bulletin board and showcase artist can usually transform any idea or advertising campaign into an appealing board or showcase. The most common inspirations for the boards and showcases in this book are generated from shopping; television ads and programs; newspaper ads and stories; advertisements; garage sales; flea markets; current trends and fads (often the products from this category are not used over and over because these trends and fads do not last long); catalogs; collections (personal ones of staff and students); home; unlikely places; the Internet; and brainstorming. Ideas are triggered from a multitude of sources; do not be limited by the usual concepts. For example, a background of hearts was combined with a student's collection of stuffed toy monkeys and gorillas reading favorite books in the showcase. Adding Spanish moss, artificial leaf garlands, plastic ferns, and indoor-outdoor carpeting was all that was needed to create a jungle setting for an unorthodox variation of the Valentine slogan, "Read to Your Sweetheart." The mind must be kept open to the possibility of ideas cropping up anywhere.

SHOPPING

Go shopping. "Shop 'til you drop" and never run out of ideas. Go to the hobby shops, toy stores, craft stores, any store, and OBSERVE. Stroll down those sale aisles. Search for something that is unique. Take those advertising banners and aisle teasers; twist them and bend the slogans into something about reading or a theme for the teacher's subject area. Be open to ideas while shopping. End-of-season sales are a good source for wallpaper and wrapping paper that can be used for backgrounds. Holiday decorations and inexpensive toys such as plastic rakes, tools, inflatable skeletons, and more are often found at the end-of-season sales. Start collecting anything that suggests a theme, such as the toy rake ("Rake in a Good Book"); toy shovel ("Dig into Reading—or Math, English, Science"); toy bugs ("Buggy About Books"); and toy grasshoppers ("Hop into Reading"). These are just a few ideas and suggestions of items that can be found while shopping and then used to create an eye-catching board. A postseason sale on costumes for dolls inspired a *Wizard of Oz* showcase; once the costumes were bought, very few other items had to be purchased. The pastel background and green burlap in this showcase were from the basic supplies list. An inexpensive piece of yellow vinyl was bought to make the yellow brick road. It was cut to show perspective, and bricks were drawn on using a Sharpie pen. One small bouquet of silk poppies was disassembled to make a field of poppies by sticking the individual flowers into the burlap. The "Emerald City" was created inexpensively from rolled tubes of newspaper and sprayed with green paint. These tubes were then sprinkled with glitter and glued together. Cotton batting from the basic supplies list was pulled apart to create a "mist" around the city. This showcase was quite popular and it sprang into being with finds of doll costumes on sale. Shopping generates hundreds of ideas and costs nothing if ideas are all that are gained. Often, the ideas come and then useful items lying around the house or school are recruited to implement them. Yes, shopping could be expensive if one is a compulsive shopper, but many shopping trips have inspired themes that utilized existing props in the library, classrooms, or home.

TELEVISION

Of course, there is no better source of ideas for capitalizing on the love of reading than the television. Popular television shows create an interest that, if teachers and librarians are able to duplicate it, can attract students and keep their love of reading going strong. Examples of this technique are numerous: "Tool Time" easily becomes "Tool Time Reading" using hammers, screwdrivers, pliers, and other tools for props and highlighting the woodworking and carpentry books from the library. The possibilities are limitless. While channel surfing, pay attention to ads. Commercials such as "Like a Rock" for Chevy trucks easily jogs the mind into creating the slogan "Rocky Reading," which features books on rocks and geology, or it could easily become "Reading Rocks" featuring the rock music books. Cultivate the ability to capitalize on the opportunity that television offers for finding unique and appealing ideas when the mind is trained to look for them.

NEWSPAPERS

Newspapers generate a multitude of ideas for boards and showcases. Play a mental game by selecting any advertisement and transforming it into an advertisement for reading or subject content. "Moonlight Madness" sales are featured throughout the year in the newspaper. This theme logically leads into use in October with a huge, orange harvest moon, the generic showcase tree with an owl or skeleton sitting in it, and the transformed slogan, "Moonlight Reading Madness" featuring mysteries or horror books. Play this mental game to train the brain, often, to find new and unique ideas that the students have not seen in every classroom or library. Notice the want ads and sports sections of the newspapers. Often catchy phrases and some of the best descriptive writing is found in the sports page: "Spartans Roll Over Cowboys" could easily inspire a perceptive librarian into featuring new books and naming the board "Roll into the Library for a New Book."

ADVERTISEMENTS

Advertisements in newspapers, stores, magazines, the Internet, road sign bill boards, airports, shopping malls, television, and anywhere inspire slogans. Be observant to see if these ads can be scrambled, realigned, or redesigned to become a bulletin board or showcase message. Retail stores receive coordinated sales and ad campaigns at least four times a year during each of the four seasons. Repeat and reword these slogans to emphasize reading and other curriculum needs. Target reading, just like the advertising pros target their markets, to inspire students to become lifetime readers.

GARAGE SALES

Garage sales are an excellent source for ideas. Artificial plants, flower arrangements, toys and props can be disassembled and used repeatedly in a variety of combinations. One never knows what great inexpensive discovery is lurking at a garage sale. A miniature stove ("Hot Reading"), cowboy boots ("Boot-Scootin' Books"), a sewing machine ("Books Are Sew Good"), toy animals, and endless other cast-off treasures can be utilized when purchased with a theme in mind. Buy inexpensive racquets, golf clubs, and ball bats for the board and showcase featured in this book, "Swing into Spring Reading." Make a resolution to explore garage sales when looking for props or ideas.

CURRENT TRENDS AND FADS

Current trends are indispensable sources for ideas. Slogans from the summer's hottest movie often make great back-to-school boards. A Terminator movie poster had the slogan, "I'm Back!" "I'm" was changed to "We're Back!"; then "To Reading" was added. Posters from movies make simple and easy bulletin boards to construct, and the students are glad to see something or someone they like inviting them to enjoy books and reading. Storage drawers and cabinets are filled with the same old back-to-school red apples, same old yellow buses, pencils, rulers, and schoolhouses. None of them inspires reading. Many of these cardboard items have been seen so many times in each of the students' classes since kindergarten that they have become invisible. Students just do not see them or pay any attention to them by the time they get to the secondary school level. Today's students need something they like to grab their attention. Rock stars, sports stars, Internet themes, and body piercing may be in and out, but there are always things and people that inspire students. Try to focus on these likes and use them in a way that is positive for reading or subject area content. Be aware of what the current trends are and capitalize on their popularity. Displays on scary books are always a big attraction. *Star Wars* is a good example of a fad that often becomes a classic: *Star Wars* gets a lot of attention however and whenever it is chosen to be used. Students are surprised to find out that classics are not all "thick, boring books." A striking board or showcase can highlight *Dracula*, *A Connecticut Yankee in King Arthur's Court*, *Of Mice and Men*, and *The Secret Garden*, which are all favorite classics that are in constant circulation. These classics are in great demand, especially after a new movie version has been released. Do not miss the opportunity to capitalize on the current movie's popularity.

CATALOGS

Every library and teacher gets hundreds of catalogs and junk mail. Turn this junk into sources of innovative boards and showcases. Budgets often restrict how many kits and items can be purchased. Order what money allows and create the rest. Many miniature books that creatures and characters read on the boards and in the showcases featured in this book are cut out from vendor catalogs. These colorful reproductions are easily glued onto card stock and folded into a book. Students laugh at some of the titles the props are reading. The duck showcase, for example, featured the mother duck reading Art Linkletter's book, *Kids Say the Darndest Things*, while the little ducks following her were reading *High Flying, The Stealth Fighter Pilot*, and *Be an Olympic Swimmer*. Students and faculty notice this sense of humor and feel more welcome in the library. They often stop in just to remark about the humorous titles. Catalogs are a very valuable source of ideas and items for the boards and showcases.

COLLECTIONS

Almost everybody collects something; some people collect everything. Search those people out when hard-to-find objects are needed. It is amazing what can be found if a note is placed in the school paper or bulletin. Students and faculty love to see their collections being used. Many times a showcase has inspired a faculty member or student to remark, "I have a collection of eagles, or author dolls, or owls, or cows if you ever want to use them." One faculty member has offered an 18-inch Emily Dickinson doll to use. It has not been borrowed yet, but it is on the planning sheet of possibilities.

INTERNET

One source of ideas being explored more and more is the Internet. This source may become the best asset because most of the suggested resources already mentioned are now available on the Internet (even shopping.) Just type in a subject, think, brainstorm, and imagine. Thousands of sources will come up to help decide the theme or slogan. It takes time, but it is a gold mine of ideas.

BRAINSTORM

Brainstorm with fellow workers, family, student aides, and anyone who will listen. Write down slogans and ideas as they occur, no matter how far-fetched or unlikely they sound. Do not evaluate these ideas until they stop materializing. Then go back and discuss them for possible use. Keep a file by subject or theme. A simple recipe box with index cards is a convenient place to store ideas for future reference; reading through the cards can start different trains of thought. Sometimes it is very helpful to "sleep on it." The next day, one of the brainstormed ideas gels and becomes the exact one wanted, or suddenly a way is perceived to make it even more appealing.

UNLIKELY PLACES

Do not forget to expect great ideas to pop up in unlikely places. The "Un-'Bull'-ievable Books" showcase was the result of seeing a fan holding up a sign at a Chicago Bulls game that was being televised. This sighting sparked a showcase featuring a Michael Jordan doll, a miniature basketball hoop, a towel with the Bulls logo, and books about basketball. It got rave reviews by students and faculty. A fabric store selling "Boot-Scootin' " material inspired a "Boot-Scootin' Books" showcase featuring the Western genre. Student aides helped place the boots so that they appeared to be line dancing. Just talking with coworkers often produces dozens of ideas. Choose one that works. Let people know that suggestions for new designs and input are very welcome, and never forget to be thinking about themes and slogans in unlikely places.

HOME

Look around home and school for objects that tie into the selected themes. Small chunks of firewood, stuffed animals, travel souvenirs, fabric scraps, doll furniture, and old clothes are just a few of the items that have been called into service over the years. Those toys and items that are not used now, but are of too much sentimental value to discard, become the best props to use. Dig these items out of the attic and closets and make them useful.

THEME

Once an idea is generated from these different sources, a theme is the next step in developing a bulletin board display. Often the props or items automatically scream out the theme, just as the toy rake, shovel, and miniature stove did. If a theme is not obvious, start brainstorming until a theme is in place; then incorporate this theme into a slogan.

SLOGANS

The slogan should usually be short and to the point. Play word games; many times the best headline or slogan is not the first idea. An example of this game playing would be to decide to feature classic books. Finding a poster of Leonardo DiCaprio from *Romeo and Juliet* was the catalyst for this board; the theme, of course, was classic reading. Brainstorming resulted in these possible slogans: "Read a Classic," "Classic Reads," "Shakespeare Is Classic," and "Leo Recommends These Classics." Many other ideas could be generated for this board, but these are enough to illustrate this technique. "Read a Classic" was the one chosen for the headline. Often the other choices are equally motivating. Try to implement the catchiest and most thought-provoking slogan.

LAYOUT SKETCH

The next step in getting started is to make a rough layout. A small sketch is helpful to visualize the overall effect, implementing the sketch is often trial-and-error. Next, collect the items for the board or showcase. Sometimes it has taken several years to gather all the items needed to create some of the best showcases, so whenever a unique idea pops up, jot it down and start gathering the materials. Sketch the layout, and as props are procured, check them off the sketch. This technique enables organization that is beneficial and helpful in getting the final product completed.

FINAL PRODUCT

The final step is putting up the display. Remember to experiment with different arrangements by pinning the items up. When the best arrangement is chosen, staple everything to stabilize it. Stay open to new ideas, rearrangements, and wording changes as the display is constructed. The end result is often different from the preliminary sketch. The final arrangement is often the result of trial and error. Keep experimenting until the layout is pleasing and satisfactory.

COSTS

Often colleagues look at the bulletin boards and showcases and comment that they do not have the money to make their boards and showcases look like these. It is not necessary to spend a lot of money to provide exciting and challenging showcases and bulletin boards. Most of the featured items in this book have been inexpensive. If a miniature washer and dryer is not easily found, use the overhead or opaque projector to make one. Computer paper boxes are easily transformed into a washer or dryer by stapling or hot gluing a top onto the back of the box and then cutting a lid from the top or front. Paint the inside of the lid white. Many times the decision for the type of props used is determined by the librarian's or teacher's availability of money and resources. The washer and dryer used in this book was found first, and then the showcase evolved by brainstorming for the slogan. Many kits are available from library supply catalogs. Many single items are available but are often expensive. Most of the boards and showcases in this book, and often the most popular ones, are created as they are constructed.

ON-SITE CONSTRUCTION

On-site construction is often the only way to complete gathering just the right materials. One does not have to be an artist to make most items. Remember to be on the lookout for anything to illustrate good ideas and be open to whatever crops up. When the right item cannot be found, make it! An inflatable skeleton was inflated and then wrapped in strips of muslin to become a needed mummy. A scrap piece of vinyl was painted to create a teepee. If there is no washer and dryer to be found and making one does not happen, substitute a small plastic or straw laundry basket heaped with doll or baby clothes, donated or bought at garage sales. Add a child's toy ironing board and iron, and then scatter clothespins and miniature detergent boxes (found at most laundromats) to complete the wash-day scene. A scarecrow is easily made on-site by using stuffed panty hose to form a body. Two of these stuffed hose may be tied together or sewn together to make legs and arms. Next, dress the scarecrow in old clothes; the head can be sewn from scraps and stuffed or even made from a brown paper sack with the face drawn on with markers. Finish the scarecrow by gluing on yarn or raffia for hair. Another option for the face would be to sew it out of muslin and embroider a face for a more permanent addition to the prop stock. When the scarecrow is not used in the showcase, it makes a perfect addition to a display of fall or horror books when placed at the end of the book shelves in the library. Tornadoes are easily made from quilt stuffing or batting. These are just a few ideas of needed items that were produced by on-site construction.

PLANNING SHEETS

A planning sheet is convenient, both for a record of displays used and as an ongoing idea planner. Two different planning sheets have been developed to easily show what has been featured. The planning sheet for each month has room for 17 years. It is easy to see when a board was featured. Also included is a yearly plan sheet; brainstorming usually fills the margins with ideas for the year. Boards and showcases are rotated so that the students never see them more than once during their secondary school years. Exceptions are made for certain showcases that students request and ask to be put back up, but generally a board or showcase is never used again until the youngest class that saw it first has graduated. Many of the same props are used over with different slogans and headlines. Sample plan sheets are included in Chapter Four. These plan sheets are very helpful and the librarian or teacher can readily decide if enough time has elapsed between usage of the boards. It is suggested that pencil be used on planning sheets, because many times current events or local programs require rapid changes in these plans.

THEME CATEGORIES

Suggestions to feature for boards and showcases include different genres of literature; local color and interests; contests; weather; travel; hobbies; special events; current events; sports; month-by-month events; and miscellaneous.

LITERARY GENRES

The different genres of literature spark student interest when featured in the showcase or on bulletin boards. These genres may be featured any time of the year, although some definitely complement the different seasons, for example, mysteries and horror for fall and Halloween. Be sure to develop boards and displays for these genres: Science Fiction, Fantasy, Historical Fiction, Romance, Sports, Horror, Mysteries, Westerns, Travel, Biographies, and Classics.

LOCAL COLOR AND INTERESTS

Most communities have festivals and parades that feature local color and themes of local interests. Green Corn Festivals, Pumpkin Festivals, and Herb-and-Plant Festivals are just a few hosted locally in this area. These local activities are great ways to promote reading and increase public awareness and public relations. The *Phantom of the Opera* board and showcase is great for October, but was also used when *Phantom of the Opera* toured neighboring cities. The Egyptian showcase would be appropriate any time, but especially when the King Tut and other Egyptian exhibits are touring nearby. Be certain to capitalize on these opportunities of local interests.

CONTESTS

Contest boards and showcases are very popular items. Anything that allows participation from the students draws interest. Contests attract students, faculty, and staff and are usually held in conjunction with National Library Week in April. The "How Many . . . ?" contests can be a hit. "Books: The Key to Success" features books on testing, education, and scholarships. It challenges the participants to guess how many keys are in the showcase. Students are lured into the contest by a blue-and-gold wrapping-paper background accented with big "brass" (plaster) keys. Sitting in the middle of the showcase is the ever-useful pedestal supporting a clear plastic container (used to hold candy in the concession stand) full of old, discarded keys borrowed from the local locksmith. Prizes for the closest guess to the correct number of keys in the container are awarded to a junior high student, a senior high student and a faculty or staff member. Other successful contest promotions include "How Many Books in the Showcase?" and "How Many Cups of Popped Corn in the Bag?"

WEATHER

Weather is always fascinating to students, perhaps because it changes so often, affects lives so much, cannot be controlled, and is rarely predicted. Do not overlook the occasion to use the weather to promote reading excitement. For example: "Winter Brings Good Knights to Read" (using knights and castles); "Warm Up with Reading" (a snowman reading a book); and "Be Cool This Summer . . . Read" (cool cat reading amid a beach scene) are just a few weather examples. "Fan-tastic Books for Summer" is a May bulletin board that has been used more than once with positive results. It encourages summer reading and gives book suggestions. April showers, March winds, and spring fever are all great weather themes to be featured.

TRAVEL

Travel themes are popular and capture student interest in geography and traveling throughout the world. Theme boards and showcases attract the students' attention with the use of catchy puns and eye-grabbing displays. "Book an Adventure" has been a successfully repeated theme, varying the destination. A trip to the Orient incorporates travel posters, fans, dolls, a kimono, and floral background with a display of books about the Orient and origami. Australia can be highlighted with koala bears hanging onto the generic library tree decorated with eucalyptus leaves.

HOBBIES

Hobby themes always get comments from students and especially from the young men who sometimes never say anything. Fishing is very popular in this area of the country, and a fishing theme stops traffic outside the library. The fish that hook their attention may be found at the local fabric store. A printed block of material depicting fish is cut out, sewn, and stuffed. Then the resulting stuffed fish are hung from a stringer or posed jumping at a lure. Pictures or cutouts of fish can be substituted for the cloth ones. Stuffed fish are also available for purchase at various retail stores. Fishing poles and a hat complement the fishy wrapping paper background.

A display of books on fishing and science books about fish complete the theme, "Get Hooked on Reading." This theme could be used as "Get Hooked on Math" (English, History, or whatever the subject may be). Use formulas, adjectives, or dates for the lures and transfer the idea to a bulletin board. A dowel rod and string make a fine fishing pole for a board display. Other hobbies such as racing, bird watching, boating, and skiing could easily be featured and will be guaranteed traffic stoppers.

SPECIAL EVENTS

Special events should be featured to include areas that sometimes do not fit into other categories. National months, multicultural events, and the Olympics fit into this area. The Summer and Winter Olympics, the elections, the Gulf War, Miss America and her platform, or graduation all present themes for display. Incorporate newspaper articles, posters, and items found around the house to effectively highlight these subjects. During the Gulf War, the daily news releases, along with a laminated map published in the local newspaper, were posted. The title of the board was "Read All About It," and it attracted both adults and students. Multicultural commemorations such as Deaf Awareness Week, Native American History Month, and Women's History Month are good selections for their respective dates. Remember to include National Library Week in April.

SPORTS

When featuring sports and sports teams, consider using their team colors for the background on the boards and showcases. One might use red and black for the Chicago Bulls and blue and gray for the Dallas Cowboys. Posters of current sports stars are always available at local retail shops. Students also stop to take notice of their favorite pro stars reading. Many sports figures have also made the READ posters for the American Library Association (ALA). These stars are very important to the students. Often, the most reluctant readers cannot resist a board or showcase that features their favorite sports star. Make the most of the influence that sports play in the life of the secondary school student. Use this influence to capture those reluctant readers into checking out a book to read about their favorite sports stars. Such readers will usually return for another book once they are hooked.

SOURCES OF PROPS

Sources of items to help with showcases and bulletin boards are found in kits, picture files, commercial kits, posters, coloring books, magazines, old greeting cards, discarded books and workbooks, art and woodworking departments, donations, and from government agencies.

KITS

Complete bulletin board kits are available for purchase from several library companies. A list of vendors is listed in the Suggested Resources at the end of Chapter Four. Most of these kits furnish flat items and props. Do not forget that these captions and slogans are usable in new creations, too. The convenience of having a kit ready to slap up on the board is a plus. Experience has shown that these kits do not attract the interest and comments of the students and faculty as much as the three-dimensional ones featured in this book. However, many scheduling conflicts, peak usage times, and life in general have proven the need to have something that can be put up at a moment's notice. These kits are invaluable tools to have on hand for these emergencies. After librarians and teachers have created several of the boards and showcases in this book, they will notice that they have in fact created their own kits with three-dimensional objects. These kits are not available for purchase and are not seen everywhere. Just as it is never a chosen scenario to appear at a social gathering and find several people wearing the same apparel; it is also not appealing to have every classroom and library decorated with the same bulletin board. Be unique.

POSTERS

Posters attract a lot of student attention. Posters of rock stars, cars, pets, and other items of popular interest are also available for purchase. Captions that stress reading can be written or typed and enlarged on the copier or computer. Then these captions can be taped onto or around the posters. Examples of posters used successfully for bulletin boards are many. One successful usage was a poster picturing a dalmation sitting in front of a chalkboard filled over and over with "I will not bark in class." This poster was transformed into a reading awareness poster by adding a balloon caption that stated, "I shoulda been reading!" Strips of paper with names of helpful reading matter such as *The Student Handbook*, *Rules*, and *Emily Post's Book of Etiquette* were placed strategically around the poster. Another successful poster portrayed a shar pei dog wearing glasses, hair curlers, and an old housedress; the shar pei was ironing. There was no caption, so the caption, "Get a Life . . . Read" was added. This poster caused the students to stop, laugh, and comment about it. It got their attention and, perhaps, planted the idea that a person who reads has a more meaningful life. Another popular poster pictured three shar pei puppies wearing baby bonnets and standing up in a baby bed with the slogan, "Rise and Whine." The slogan, "It's Reading Time" was added and transformed these babies into reading promoters. Mickey Mouse wallpaper was chosen for the background and made the puppies look as if they were in a nursery. Posters add a lot of fun. Some posters cannot be resisted because they are so cute. Their use to promote and stress reading and other curriculum areas is very beneficial to the students.

PATTERNS

Colleagues and students constantly ask, "Where did you get that?" If items are not easily found and must be made for the showcase, new problems arise. Where is an easily reproduced pattern of the object to be found? There are many resources. Coloring books are excellent sources because they have dark, clean lines and project well on the wall when using the overhead projector. The simpler the drawing, the easier it is to reproduce. Clip art on CD-ROM, the Internet, and in books also make excellent sources for patterns. Cutouts from old greeting cards, newspapers, magazines, discarded books, coloring books, and workbooks can be used to obtain patterns to use for the bulletin boards and showcases. Using these patterns and the opaque projector to enlarge them on paper, cardboard, fake fur, and other materials results in soft sculptures and items that complete unique displays. Other sources of patterns can be found in picture files, government agencies, and commercial shops. Often, the art and woodworking department will collaborate on artwork and patterns. Be certain to give plenty of advance notice when working with these groups. The illustrations of the bulletin boards and showcases in Chapter Three will make excellent patterns to use on the opaque projector.

DONATIONS

Get the word out that donations of props and items are needed and accepted. After an Egyptian showcase was featured, a perfect reproduction of a Nefertiti bust with an accompanying podium and Plexiglas cover was donated to the school system. The administration left it housed in the library, where it will make a priceless addition to the next Egyptian showcase. In the meantime, Nefertiti reigns over the library and sparks many a study in researching her life and times. It is amazing what may find its way to the library when the patrons, public, and staff become aware of its needs.

Chapter Three

Finished Products

ow is the time to assemble the bulletin boards, displays, and showcases. But first, a few explanations, descriptions, and helpful hints for following the instructions for the construction of showcases and bulletin boards should be discussed. Dimensions and lengths of props for the displays are purposely left out in most cases because boards and showcases come in all sizes. Always measure material before cutting or buying to be certain that enough has been purchased.

TREE

The tree displayed in many of the showcases is just a tree limb picked up from the yard. Find one that is approximately as tall as the showcase in which it is going to be used. As the seasons change, so does this tree. Green leaves are taped, stapled, or pinned to it to create a summer or springtime tree. Fall leaves are similarly fastened to it to change the season to autumn. Cotton batting is laid on its branches to evoke a snowy day. Animals cling to its branches, sit in it, read in it and under it. Its use is unlimited. Placing the tree in the foreground of the showcase gives extra dimension and texture to the display. Placing the tree in a back corner gives the illusion of extra depth. Move the tree around. Try different placements to vary the showcase appearance and scenery.

SLINGS

The sling is a support used to display books on the showcase walls and bulletin boards. Use of the sling enables using real books instead of book jackets. Book jackets may then be left on the book to protect it. These strips of material, string, ribbon, or laminating film make it possible to display the actual books in attractive arrangements without damaging the volume. Cut a strip about one inch wide from the selected material. Cut a strip about five to ten inches long, depending upon the size of the book. It is desirable to have approximately two inches extra for each book so that this excess may be stapled to the board. Staple the ends of the strip to the background horizontally or at a slight angle where desired. Either insert the bottom corner of the book behind the strip as far down as possible, or open the book and insert half the pages behind the sling as if it was a bookmark. Larger volumes may need a wider, stronger material. Examples of these two slings can be seen in the displays "What Are You Cut Out to Be?" and "Vote to Read."

RUBBER CEMENT

This versatile adhesive turns any lightweight object into a seemingly suspended item simply by applying a dab of it to the object and pressing it against the inside of the glass showcase door, window, or directly to the laminated background of the bulletin board. Raindrops fall, snowflakes drift, fish swim, stars shine, butterflies flutter, and bugs buzz at eye level right before the eyes of the students; the cement is invisible. This technique adds more dimension and flair to the scene. When the display is dismantled, gently pull off the rubber cement and rub any residue off the glass. This technique works best if the item is laminated or of a nonporous material, such as aluminum foil raindrops or stars. Items may be created by using an opaque projector, computer clip art, a die-cutting machine, or freehand cuttings.

FLOORING

Carpet strips cut to the exact size of the showcase floor give a finishing touch to the scene being created. Artificial turf can set an outdoor theme. Cut a second piece of artificial turf; touch it up with dabs of brown, red, orange, and gold paint; it then becomes an autumn ground cover. White carpet turns the scene into winter. If the base is already wood, take advantage of that for indoor exhibits and use it as a base for a small throw rug or make it into a gym floor. Use those vacation sea shells to create a beach scene! Be innovative!

SHOWCASE CEILING

Items may be suspended by hanging them on fishing line, which is taped to the surface if the showcase has a solid ceiling. This technique gives the illusion of birds in flight or snowflakes falling, or it supports an ivy vine twisting itself across the case. If the ceiling has movable tiles or light cover, take advantage of the support strips to hang various props. A length of coat hanger cut to fit between the supports is used as a beam from which different lengths of fishing line with props are tied. By employing two or more of these rods, it becomes possible to suspend everything: snowflakes, leaves, sports rackets, animals, holiday ornaments, and anything else imaginable.

SPECIAL EFFECTS

A cloud background can be created from a package of computer paper printed with a cloud design. The sheets are taped together in strips the width of the bulletin board and also in widths to fit the showcase. Then these strips are laminated. Another source for special effects is wrapping paper with similar cloud designs and items such as stars, snowflakes, and lightning, which enhance outdoor theme boards and showcases.

If large rolls of art craft paper are available at your school, cut pieces in various colors to fit the width of the board and the showcase background. These pieces are then cut in half lengthwise and laminated. The strips are now ready to be cut freehand into strips of green grass, blue waves, white drifts of snow, or brown hills.

Small pieces of Styrofoam may be used in order to produce a three-dimensional effect on bulletin boards and showcases. Save Styrofoam scraps for this purpose. Little squares may be glued to the backs of letters, stars, leaves, or miniature book covers to give depth to the display. Larger strips or blocks turn a napkin into a tablecloth on a table or make a character stand out from the board. Foam packing can become "popcorn" when put into small sacks or boxes obtained from a concession stand. Strips of Styrofoam may be purchased or found in packing materials. Using foam board to create props also adds dimension and alleviates the boredom of flat objects. A tip to remember about cutting Styrofoam is to rub the knife on a candle to coat it with wax; and it will then be able to slice through the Styrofoam without having to saw.

ELEVATION

Sometimes it is desirable to elevate the showcase displays to achieve the correct eye level and to center props and slogans to add interest or highlight a theme. Use books or boxes as a platform by making level or unequal stacks to the height or heights needed. Cover the stacks with draped material to create the desired effect. Green burlap simulates a grassy hill, white velvet or cotton batting portrays snow drifts, while black trash bags against a black background set an eerie mood.

The individual size of showcases determines the need for elevation. The size of props also determines when to implement elevation and different elevations. When fashion dolls or small collectible items are used, elevation becomes very important.

TITLES:

> *Get Back into the Swing of Reading*
> *Swing into Reading*
> *Swinging Reads*

BACKGROUND: Red paper

BORDERS: "Book" printed border (purchased) or solid coordinating border

LETTERINGS: White pin backs; cutouts; computer-produced banner

PROPS: Small, old-fashioned board swing in a size proportionate to the board; leafy vines; rag doll or any doll that fits into the swing; miniature book; list of suggested reading titles; rope; artificial apple

INSTRUCTIONS: Staple background to board. Staple border around edges. Make a swing by drilling holes in a section of 2x4 board. Thread rope through the holes and knot it under the board so it will not pull out, or pass the rope up through the holes from under the swing, leaving the ends free to fasten to the board. Hang swing from the top left corner of the board, prop it in position with pushpins. Wrap the leafy vines around the rope. Secure the doll on the swing by pinning through it or its clothes to the bulletin board with T-pins. Staple the slogan onto the right side of the board or use the pin back letters to spell the slogan. Staple the reading list to the board under the slogan. Attach a miniature book to the doll's hands with tape or pins. Fasten artificial apple to the swing with tape.

TITLES:

*Get Back into the Swing of
   Reading*
Swing into Reading
Swinging Books
Swing into College-Bound Reading

BACKGROUND: Blue sky paper

BORDERS: None

FLOORING: Artificial green turf

LETTERINGS: White pin backs;
cutouts; computer-produced banner

PROPS: Small old-fashioned board
swing in a size proportionate to the
showcase; leafy vines; rag doll or any
doll that can be made to sit in the
swing; leaves; suggested college-
bound books stacked up and tied
with a belt or book strap; books to
scatter around floor; rope; tree limb; artificial apples; sack lunch; miniature book

INSTRUCTIONS: Staple background to wall of showcase. Put artificial turf on the floor of
showcase. Put the tree limb in the showcase. Make a swing by drilling holes in a section of 2x4
board. Thread rope through the holes and knot it under the board so it won't pull out, or pass the
rope up through the holes from under the swing, leaving the ends free to fasten to the tree or
showcase. Hang swing from the top left side of the showcase with wire, or staple to ceiling. If this
arrangement is not possible, hang it from the top of the showcase by using T-pins and attach it to
the back wall of the showcase. Another option would be to hang the swing from the branches of
the tree by taping it to the limbs or pinning it to the limbs. Secure the doll on the swing by pinning its hands with T-pins to the ropes. Tape an open book to the doll's hands. Staple the slogan
onto the right side of the back wall or use the pin back letters to spell out the slogan. Put the
college-bound reading books into a stack. Buckle a belt or book strap around them. Place them in
the lower right side of the showcase floor. Put the lunch on top of the stack of books. Scatter
more books in the floor of the showcase where needed. Place artificial apples around the books, in
the swing, and even in the tree. These apples are available in after-Christmas sales or in the artificial fruit section of craft stores. Put leaves on the tree by stapling, taping, or wrapping leafy vines
around the tree limbs. Wrap the ropes of the swing with leafy vines.

TITLES:

Back to Books Time
Reading Is Timeless
Time to Read

BACKGROUND: School colors or fancy wallpaper

BORDERS: Gold border

LETTERINGS: Pin backs or cutouts

PROPS: Pictures of clocks and watches cut out of magazines, as big as possible, and as many as needed to make an attractive arrangement (could make with aid of the opaque projector); real battery-powered wall clocks (borrow from home and faculty)

INSTRUCTIONS: Staple background and border to board. Center title. Hang clocks or illustrations of clocks around the title as shown.

VARIATIONS: Buy party favors of plastic watches at party or toy stores. Staple them to board or use them to make a unique and timely border of watches. Staple old *Time* magazines or book titles with "time" in the titles to the board.

TITLES:

Back to Books Time
Reading Is Timeless
Time to Read

BACKGROUND: Sky blue or wrapping paper with cloud pattern or solid color of choice

BORDERS: None

FLOORING: Artificial green turf

LETTERINGS: Pin backs or cutouts

PROPS: Big Ben 3-D Puzzle or tall real clock; real clocks and watches; wall clocks; cotton-batting clouds; books with "Time" in the titles

INSTRUCTIONS: Staple the background to the walls of the showcase. Put in the artificial turf flooring. Put in the model of Big Ben or a tall clock. May substitute more clocks or a travel poster of Big Ben if the model is not available. Arrange books around the base of the clock and in the floor of the showcase. Hang the other clocks on the walls. Set clocks to different times to emphasize that any time is "time to read."

VARIATIONS: Use posters of clocks or travel posters of Big Ben. Cardboard clocks from the elementary grades that are used to teach students how to tell time might be borrowed to complete showcase. Real watches and small alarm clocks could be scattered among the books, on the side walls, and on the floor of the showcase to complete the theme.

TITLES:

Whale-come Back to Reading
Whale of a Tale
Whale Tales

BACKGROUND: Light blue or sky with clouds for top portion; three layers of blue waves on a deeper blue paper for the lower portion.

BORDERS: None used

LETTERINGS: Black four inch cut outs

PROPS: Blue craft paper or blue fabric cut into three strips of "waves;" black whale tail cut from paper (either draw freehand or enlarge this picture using the opaque projector)

INSTRUCTIONS: Staple light blue or cloud background on upper portion of the board. Layer the wave strips across the bottom half of the board. Insert the whale tail into the middle strip of waves. Staple letters in two rows across the top of the board.

VARIATIONS: A row of die-cut fish or whales with book titles printed on them could be added across the bottom wave. A reading list of books on topics such as whales, marine life, and oceans could be posted.

TITLES:

Whale-come Back to Reading
Books to Spout About
Whale Tales

BACKGROUND: Whale fabric; blue cloud paper; wrapping paper with ocean scenes.

BORDERS: None

FLOORING: Solid royal blue fabric

LETTERINGS: Black four-inch cutouts

PROPS: Toy stuffed whale; sea shells; plastic crab, lobster, starfish (bought at a hobby store); books with whale or marine themes

INSTRUCTIONS: Staple the background to the walls of the showcase. Center and staple the slogan. Build up the showcase floor with books, boxes, or crumpled newspaper. Cover these lumps with dark blue fabric. Pin the stuffed whale to the back wall. Prop an opened book in front of him so he looks as if he is reading. Scatter the sea shells, starfish, lobster, crab, and other sea creatures around the whale. Prop open books in front of the larger creatures so they also look as if they are reading. Place other books about whales and marine life around the props to balance the arrangement.

VARIATIONS: Create whales and sea creatures by using the opaque projector.

TITLES:

Welcome Back to Royal Treatment in the Library
The Royalty of Reading
Royal Reads
Reading Reigns

BACKGROUND: Solid royal blue or purple paper or satin material

BORDERS: Gold

LETTERINGS: Gold cutouts or white pin backs

PROPS: Five crowns of various shapes and sizes. These crowns may be purchased from party supply stores or they are easily made. Burger King, at one time, gave free crowns to children, and may be a source for these props.

INSTRUCTIONS: Staple paper and border to the board. Staple slogan in the center of the board. Staple crowns as shown in the illustration.

VARIATIONS: Write titles about King Arthur, castles, medieval times, and fairy tales on strips of paper or on shapes of crowns or castles. Substitute pictures, die cuts, or patterns of castles for crowns.

TITLES:

*Welcome Back to Royal Treatment
in the Library
In Days of Old When Knights
Were Bold . . . Read About It!
"Knightly" Reading*

BACKGROUND: Blue and gold fancy wrapping paper or solid royal blue or purple paper

BORDERS: Gold or royal blue

FLOORING: Velvet or off-white material folded or draped across the floor

LETTERINGS: Gold or white pin backs

PROPS: Banner with knight or castle motif (purchased or created from poster board or fabric); velvet material to drape or fold attractively for bottom of showcase; knight model; suit of armor model (purchase or make one from cardboard with aid of the opaque projector); antique gold books or books about knights, castles, etc.; jewelry such as antique brooches, ornate rings; old coins or fake coins; a king's robe; crown; glass jewels found in craft departments; toy sword

INSTRUCTIONS: Staple background and border onto showcase walls. Put material in floor or make mounds and folds. Hang banner in upper left corner of the showcase. Place the knight's suit of armor or other collected royal objects strategically around the showcase. Put the king's robe and crown on the knight. Place the toy sword and books at eye-appealing spaces around the knight and banner. Place the glass jewels, jewelry, and old coins strategically around books and other objects.

VARIATIONS: Many inexpensive party favors that are available at retail outlets could add to this showcase if some of these items are hard to find. Substitute anything that seems appropriate. Be innovative.

TITLES:

Kick Off the Year to a Good Start . . . Read!
Kick Off the Season with Books
Get a Kick Out of Reading

BACKGROUND: School and team colors

BORDERS: School and team colors

LETTERINGS: Pin back or four-inch cutouts

PROPS: "Leg" drawn on poster board, foam core poster board, or Styrofoam colored with markers in school uniform colors, or an athletic sock stuffed to make a leg; shoe (real soccer or football shoe . . . check with coaches for an extra); football, soccer ball, a poster board cut out of a football, or a partially deflated real ball

INSTRUCTIONS: Staple the background to the board. Place a small piece of Styrofoam (this gives the leg the appearance of standing out from the wall) behind the leg, then staple the leg at the edge of the bulletin board. Staple the border around the edges of the bulletin board. Pin the shoe to the bulletin board using T-pins. Place the foot of the leg into the shoe. Attach lettering. Angle the ball so that it looks as if it has been kicked. Secure ball with staples or T-pins.

VARIATIONS: Add book titles about sports or make a list of sports books.

TITLES:

Get A Kick Out of Reading
Kick Off the Year to a Good
    Start...Read!
Fall Kick Off of Books

BACKGROUND: School and team colors

BORDERS: None

FLOORING: Artificial turf with fall colors painted on and mixed with the green

LETTERINGS: Contrasting school color pin back or four-inch cutouts

PROPS: Stuffed dummy, large doll, or large stuffed animal (be innovative and use a stuffed animal mascot, for example, a bear if the team is named the Bears); dress the character in a soccer uniform or football jersey and helmet; soccer or football shoes; soccer ball, football, or Styrofoam ball painted like a soccer ball (could also use a cutout of ball); books about fall sports; autumn leaves; school pennant; spirit ribbons and buttons; green strip of grass background; sports water bottle

INSTRUCTIONS: Staple background to walls of the showcase. Staple the green grass strip around the base. Put artificial turf in the bottom of the showcase. Fasten dressed figure to the back wall of the case with T-pins, pushpins, or staples. Arrange the legs so that they appear to be kicking the ball. An old soccer ball or the football could be partially deflated and hung on the wall. A Styrofoam ball could be cut in half, painted like a soccer ball, and pinned to the wall. Arrange books and leaves around the floor. Pin the slogan above the figure. Staple a school pennant above the slogan and one on the left side of it. Spirit ribbons and school spirit buttons may be added to the walls and scattered among the books. Place a sports water bottle on top of the books as illustrated.

TITLES:

Bounce into the Library—Be Bold and Read All Those Fab ulous and Cheer ful Books or Surf the Net!
Get Down to Biz! Bounce into the Library and Read All the Fab ulous Books!
Surf the Net at the Library!

BACKGROUND: Solid yellow or plaid contact or wrapping paper

BORDERS: Red

LETTERINGS: Six soap boxes plus pin backs or cutouts to finish slogan

PROPS: Clothesline; clothespins; six miniature or full-size soap boxes (Bounce, Bold, All, Fab, Cheer, and Surf); paperback books; doll clothes or small children's clothes

INSTRUCTIONS: Staple background and border to board. Plaid contact paper with the backing left on adds to the eye appeal of this layout, but solid colors from the basic supply lists will work well, too. Pin the soap boxes and pin back letters to the top three-fourths of the board. String the clothesline and staple or pin it into place. Using clothespins hang the doll clothes and light-weight paperback books.

VARIATIONS: If "Surf the Net" is chosen, use computer posters or drawings to accompany the slogan.

TITLES:

Overloaded? Read and Relax!
Clean Up Your Study Skills…Read!
Dash to the Library for Fab ulous Books!

BACKGROUND: Plain or plaid paper or fabric

BORDERS: None

FLOORING: None, carpet, or linoleum

LETTERINGS: Pin backs or cutouts (any color to coordinate with background)

PROPS: Clothesline; clothespins; doll or baby clothes; small plastic basket piled with clothes; small boxes of detergent; fabric softener; pushpins; thumbtacks; cotton batting suds running out of washer; miniature washer and dryer or toy washer and dryer (or construct one from boxes); small doll chair; small doll; small toy dog or cat; books

INSTRUCTIONS: Staple background to the walls of the showcase. Attach slogan to the back wall of the showcase. Pin up clothesline. Hang clothes on the line across the board without obscuring the slogan. Place the washer and dryer in the lower left side of the showcase. Have clothes stuffed in and falling out of the washer and cotton-batting suds coming out of the dryer. Add small books coming out of the washer and dryer. Put toy doll's chair in lower right corner and place a doll in it. Put the small miniature basket of doll clothes between the dryer and doll's chair. Place a small toy dog or cat by the doll's chair to add to the scene. Place extra books on the floor and anywhere needed to add to the scene. Choose titles about cleaning, washing, dirt, and stress relief.

TITLES:

Boot Scootin' Books
Ranch-Style Readin'
How About a Western?

BACKGROUND: Solid red or bandanna print fabric

BORDERS: Black

LETTERINGS: Black four-inch cutouts

PROPS: Boots (real, cutouts, or cardboard ones bought at local paper and party stores); titles of Westerns written or taped onto the boots; paper strips with captions as illustrated

INSTRUCTIONS: Staple background and border to the board. If real boots are used, use T-pins to pin them to the board. If boots are on loan and not discarded ones, they could be secured by putting T-pins by the heel or tying them with fishing line to hang them. Arrange the boots as if they are line dancing as illustrated. Arrange and staple the slogan. Attach to or write book titles on the boots. Attach the paper strips with captions as illustrated.

VARIATIONS: Add bandanna print neckerchiefs and other Western props as desired.

TITLES:

Boot Scootin' Books
Rodeo Reading
Two-Step on In and Read a Western

BACKGROUND: Bandanna print fabric

BORDERS: Black

FLOORING: Leaves, wood floor, or carpet

LETTERINGS: Black cutouts

PROPS: Boots from garage sales or borrowed from students or faculty; or pattern could be enlarged on poster board, colored, and cut out in different styles; computer-printed phrases as illustrated; spurs; rope; small bale of hay; Western books

INSTRUCTIONS: Staple background and border to walls of showcase. Build up bottom of the showcase with boxes. Cover the boxes with bandanna material. Use T-pins to arrange boots as if line dancing. Staple the slogan to the back wall. Staple printed phrases on background and pin to front of display as illustrated. Place a small bale of hay in the lower right corner. Place books, spurs, rope and other Western memorabilia around the boots. Scatter loose straw around boots and books. Hang the rope lariat on one of the side walls. Use slings to add more Westerns to side walls as needed for balance.

VARIATIONS: Use a mixture of rain boots, fashion boots, and hiking boots. Small cowboy hats or real cowboy hats could be scattered and stapled around.

TITLES:

What Are You Cut Out to Be?
Who Are You Cut Out to Be?
Cut Out a Career! Be on the Cutting Edge of Career Choices

BACKGROUND: Black

BORDERS: Newspaper border (purchased) or made from newsprint

LETTERINGS: Pin backs or four-inch cutouts from want ads

PROPS: Four 22-inch-tall paper dolls cut from newsprint; circle a few "choice" ads in red. Laminate. Make two males and two females or four unisex paper dolls. Four career reading lists with call numbers

INSTRUCTIONS: Staple background to board. Staple dolls to board, feet flush with bottom of the board. Staple border around the edges of the board. Attach the slogan to the board. Attach the career reading lists to the hands of the dolls.

VARIATIONS: Laminated strips of paper with different careers listed on them could add to the overall effect.

TITLES:

What Are You Cut Out to Be?
Career Cutouts
What's Cut Out for Your Future?

BACKGROUND: Red

BORDERS: Newspaper or black

FLOORING: Shredded newspaper want ads

LETTERINGS: Pin backs or cutouts in black or white; cut words "You," "Cut," and three "?"out of the classified ads

PROPS: Cut out large male and female paper dolls from the want ads; link them by the arms. Circle several of the interesting jobs in red, then laminate them for future use. Career books; slings to attach books to walls; two career reading lists with call numbers

INSTRUCTIONS: Staple background and border onto walls of the showcase. Shred newspaper want ads and spread them around the floor of the showcase. Staple slogan to the back wall. Cut out paper dolls. Glue dolls with rubber cement onto poster boards and cut them out. Laminate dolls. Make paper doll stands or staple dolls to wall of showcase. Attach the career reading lists to the hands of the dolls. Arrange career books in the shredded newsprint in the floor. Use a sling of coordinating material or fishing line to attach career books to the side walls of the showcase.

VARIATIONS: Instead of books on the side walls, two other paper dolls could be hung. Other choices would be large scissors on the walls or material with a pattern being cut out. Large strips of paper with career choices lettered on them could be attached to the walls of the showcase.

TITLES:

> *Sizzling Suspense*
> *Hot Reads*
> *Mystifying Mysteries*

BACKGROUND: Black

BORDERS: Orange

LETTERINGS: Four-inch cutouts in orange

PROPS: Large orange paper moon; small branch to make a tree; small twigs to make a stack of wood for a fire; orange and red chenille sticks for flames for a fire; cardboard or plastic cauldron or pot to put on the fire; books; strip of fall ground (orange and red tissue paper); autumn leaves; Spanish moss; small pumpkin head reader or orange paper jack-o'-lantern head; white paper or cloth for pumpkin reader body

INSTRUCTIONS: Staple background and ground strip on bottom of board. Staple border on the edges. Pin or staple small tree limb on left side of board. Staple moon behind tree limb. Staple the slogan to the board. Create a stack of wood for a fire by lashing, gluing, or tying the twigs and logs together. Staple or pin it to the lower right of the board. Make or buy a pot or cauldron. Staple it or tie it to the logs, twigs, and board. Use T-pins to secure it. Attach books behind and in the pot. Pin chenille sticks to look like steam lines coming from pot on the background. Twist orange and red chenille craft sticks around the logs. Then twist these sticks into flame shapes coming out of fire. Staple more chenille sticks around logs as needed. Attach a small pumpkin reader (made by using a pumpkin or jack-o'-lantern for the head and a piece of white sheeting for the body) under the tree and pose him reading a book. Scatter and staple fall leaves around the ground and under the tree. Drape Spanish moss on branches as needed.

VARIATIONS: List of hot reads instead of pumpkin reader. Spiderwebs and spiders could be used.

TITLES:

Sizzling Suspense
Hot Mysteries
Fiery Romances

BACKGROUND: Black garbage bags

BORDERS: None

FLOORING: Black garbage bags

LETTERINGS: Orange four-inch cutouts

PROPS: Tree limb; lighted jack-o'-lantern or real pumpkin with a drawn-on face; pedestal covered with black garbage bag for pumpkin base; plastic or real kettle or cauldron; orange and red tissue paper to scrunch up around books and between the wood in the fire; logs and limbs stacked, lashed, or tied together for the fire; orange and red chenille craft sticks to make flames for the fire; Spanish moss; orange paper moon; black bat cut-out; mystery and horror books; fall leaves

INSTRUCTIONS: Staple the background to the showcase walls. Stack books on boxes to desired height. Cover with draped black garbage bags. Place the tree limb in the case on the left side so that the branches extend across the upper part of the showcase. Staple the moon behind and between the tree limbs. Staple the bat silhouette to the moon. Staple slogan to the back wall. Drape Spanish moss on the tree. Tape a few autumn leaves on the tree. Put the pedestal in the lower left back corner of the showcase. Cover it with a black garbage bag. Place the jack-o'-lantern on the pedestal. Construct the fire from small logs and twigs. Rubber band, hot glue, or tie them into the desired shape. Scrunch tissue paper and poke it between and into the middle of the fire. Attach red and orange chenille strips to the wood and shape them into flame shapes. Place the cauldron on top of the fire. Fill it with mysteries. Scatter and arrange more sizzling suspense on the floor of the showcase. Scatter autumn leaves around the pumpkin, tree, fire, and floor of the showcase. Use slings to add mysteries to side walls if needed to fill in blank spots and balance the display.

TITLES:

Spine-Tingling Scary Books
Scary Books
Scare Up a Good Mystery
Fright Night Reading

BACKGROUND: Light orange, yellow, or black

BORDERS: None

LETTERINGS: Black or orange four-inch cutouts

PROPS: Two scarecrows approximately from 12 to 15 inches high (make or purchase at craft stores); pumpkin cutouts; ornamental corn; two cornstalks; eight darker orange pumpkin die cuts

INSTRUCTIONS: Staple background to board. Pin one scarecrow and one cornstalk to left side of board. Pin the second scarecrow and cornstalk to the right side of the board. Center slogan between the two scarecrows. Make approximately eight die-cut pumpkins from a darker orange paper. Write mystery titles on them. Staple these pumpkins under the slogan and on the bottom of the board as illustrated. Arrange ornamental corn around the slogan, scarecrows, and at the bottom of the board.

VARIATIONS: Staple mysteries on the board with slings.

TITLES:

Scary Stories
Scarecrow Reading
Scare Up a Spine Tingling Book

BACKGROUND: Golden yellow, orange, or brown

BORDERS: None

FLOORING: Autumn artificial turf

LETTERINGS: Red or white pin backs or coordinating color

PROPS: Autumn leaves; branch with fall leaves; tree limb; ornamental corn; cornstalks; large scarecrow made with child's or doll clothes; book titles with "scare" in them; large hat; glue gun; raffia; pushpins; miniature bales of hay; artificial apples

INSTRUCTIONS: Make scarecrow by stuffing clothes with newspaper, batting, or other old clothes. Hot glue raffia around inside of shirt and pant cuffs. Sew and stuff a cloth bag or stuff a paper bag for the head. Draw on features with markers. Fasten the head to the front of the scarecrow. Staple the background to the walls of the showcase. Place autumn artificial turf on the floor of the showcase. Place tree with autumn leaves in left corner of showcase. Put scarecrow leaning against the tree. Place cornstalk in right corner. Place hat on the scarecrow. Staple slogan to back of showcase wall. Put bales of hay in right corner in front of cornstalk. Place one bale standing on top of the second bale lying on its side in the lower right corner of the showcase. Place books on top of hay bales and in front of the scarecrow. Hang a branch of leaves from the ceiling of the showcase. Staple autumn leaves falling from tree limb and sky randomly on background. Scatter more leaves over scarecrow, hay, floor, and books. Place ornamental corn, cornstalks, and artificial apples by scarecrow.

TITLES:

Booooks Are Real Treats
Books Are a Treat for Your Mind
Sweet Reads

BACKGROUND: Black garbage bags

BORDERS: None

LETTERINGS: White pin backs or cutouts

PROPS: Styrofoam circles, cones, balls; orange and black tissue paper; acrylic paints (red, orange, and yellow); thin dowel sticks; newspaper for stuffing; X-ACTO knife; pins; scary book titles on strips of orange or yellow paper

INSTRUCTIONS: Staple background to board. Put up slogan. Make candy props. Paint red triangles on the Styrofoam circles so that they resemble peppermint candies. Cut cones in half lengthwise; then paint like candy corn. Insert a section of dowel into small Styrofoam balls and cover with orange tissue paper to make Tootsie pops. Cover wads of newspaper with orange and black tissue paper to make Halloween kisses candy. Arrange candies around the letters. Pin book titles onto the kisses.

TITLES:

Booooks Are Real Treats
Treats for the Mind
Treats Abound at the Library

BACKGROUND: Black garbage bags

BORDERS: Black or none

FLOORINGS: Black garbage bags

LETTERINGS: White pin backs or orange cutouts

PROPS: Twelve Styrofoam giant candy corn; four giant Halloween kisses; four Styrofoam Tootsie pops; large spiderweb; illuminated jack-o'-lantern; spiders; fall and Halloween books; ornamental corn

INSTRUCTIONS: Staple background and border to the walls of showcase. Build up floor of the showcase with books or wadded newspaper. Make the left side taller than the right. Cover these items with black garbage bags. Place the jack-o'-lantern in the tallest section on the left side of the showcase. Plug jack-o'-lantern into electrical outlet if it is available. Arrange slogan on the back wall and staple it. Suspend the spiderweb with fishing line in front of the jack-o'-lantern. Make the giant candy by following the instructions on the previous bulletin board page. Pin the candy to the walls, around the slogan, and on the sides. Place books in the foreground and on the floor. Place spiders on books. Scatter more candy corn, candy kisses, and Tootsie pops around the books. Place ornamental corn where needed for balance and eye appeal.

VARIATIONS: Suspend a ghost, a dracula doll, and other holiday items from the ceiling of the showcase. An easy ghost to create is a helium-filled balloon covered with a piece of sheeting. Attach the ghost to books with string.

TITLES:

PHANtastic Classics!
PHANtastic Reading!
PHANtastic Books!

BACKGROUND: Black

BORDERS: Black

LETTERINGS: White computer print (choose a font to fit and then enlarge it) or cutouts

PROPS: White phantom mask (purchased or cut out of poster board); long-stemmed artificial red rose; computer list (same font) of classic novels

INSTRUCTIONS: Staple background and border to the board. Staple or pin the mask in the upper left corner. Staple the rose beneath the mask. Staple the slogan to the board. Staple the computer list of classics beneath the slogan.

TITLES:

PHANtastic Classics
PHANtastic Reading
PHANtastic Books

BACKGROUND: Black satin or solid black paper or marbleized black-and-gold or black-and-white wrapping paper

BORDERS: None

FLOORINGS: Black and white satin

LETTERINGS: White computer print (choose a font to fit and then enlarge) or cutouts

PROPS: Phantom mask; a rose; a silver candelabra with candles; white gloves; white music notes; white and black satin material; white pedestal; classic books; reading list of classics; top hat

INSTRUCTIONS: Staple background to walls of showcase. Staple slogan to back wall. Pleat or drape black and white satin in the floor of the showcase. Place white pedestal in lower left side of showcase. Put candelabra on the pedestal. Fasten mask beside the slogan. Staple reading list under slogan. Place classic books in stacks and around the floor of the showcase. Place gloves, hat, and rose among these books. Sprinkle white music notes across the display. Use rubber cement to glue white music notes on the background and side walls of the showcase if so desired. Hang books using slings to the side walls to fill in blank spots to add balance to the display as needed.

VARIATIONS: Use toy piano or organ, director's baton, and opera glasses if available.

TITLES:

Vote for Reading
Vote for Books
Elect to Read

BACKGROUND: Royal blue

BORDERS: Flag border (purchased) or solid red

LETTERINGS: Four-inch red cutouts

PROPS: Five star cutouts; two 18-inch flags; list of books about elections and the Constitution; red paint or paper; two cardboard tubes approximately 12½ inches in length

INSTRUCTIONS: Staple background and border to board. Cut two tubes from center of laminating rolls or from tube mailers (approx. 12½ inches). Cover one end or stuff end lightly with newspapers. Paint red or cover with red paper. Pin to the bulletin board about four inches from each side. Put a flag in each tube. Center the slogan between each flag. Buy stars at a party or bulletin board shop or cut them out of red and white shiny wrapping paper and laminate them. Staple the stars around the flags and slogan. Staple a list of books about elections and the United States Constitution beneath the slogan.

TITLES:

Vote to Read
Elect to Read
Vote for Books
Vote for the fREADom to Read

BACKGROUND: Flag fabric or red, white, and blue plain background

BORDERS: None

LETTERINGS: Lettered on piece of paper and glued to the ballot box

FLOORINGS: Flag material continues into and covers floor

PROPS: Ballot box with slit for ballots (made out of a computer-paper box); red paper; two 24-inch American flags; ballots made from white paper; white pedestal; books; two flag holders (or two bud vases painted red or covered with red paper)

INSTRUCTIONS: Staple background material to walls of showcase. Cover the floor of the showcase with the same material. Put the pedestal in the center of the showcase. Place flag holders equidistant from the pedestal. Place flags in the flag holders. Cover ballot box and cut hole in the lid. Attach slogan to ballot box. Set ballot box on the pedestal. Use slings to hang books about elections and the Constitution, the presidents, and the government from the walls of the showcase.

VARIATIONS: Old campaign buttons, straw hats, a donkey, an elephant, and other election memorabilia could be used to further enhance the showcase. Slogan could be on the back wall of the showcase instead of on ballot box.

TITLES:

> *Rake in a Good Book*
> *Rake in Good Reading*
> *Rake in Good Reads*

BACKGROUND: Light blue background

BORDERS: None

LETTERINGS: Red letters, stencils, or cutouts

PROPS: Autumn leaves; small peck basket (or half-basket if you can find one in a hobby or craft store); child-sized rake; tree branch with leaves; strips of red, orange, and yellow paper with book titles printed on them

INSTRUCTIONS: Staple background to the board. Staple slogan to the board. Staple and pin the basket on its side on the lower left side of the board. Print book titles (by hand or by computer on red, orange, and yellow paper strips) and arrange them with the leaves as if they have fallen from the tree. Pin rake onto bulletin board with T-pins. Staple masses of leaves at the bottom.

TITLES:

Rake in a Good Book
Rake in Good Reading
Rake in Good Reads

BACKGROUND: Sky blue or cloud paper

BORDERS: None

FLOORING: Autumn artificial turf

LETTERINGS: Red cutouts

PROPS: Real rakes; small scarecrow; basket; autumn leaves; fall and fiction books with color or title-coordinated covers; tree limb; light orange material

INSTRUCTIONS: Staple background to walls of the showcase. Staple the slogan to the back wall. Put the autumn turf in the floor. Put the tree limb on the left side with angled branches going across the top of the showcase. Crumple newspaper and mound up a large triangular shape (intended to look like a huge pile of leaves) under the tree on the left. Cover the shape with light orange material. Put a basket in the right side of the showcase. Lean different types of rakes against the wall in front of the basket. Set a doll or scarecrow in the pile of leaves. Tape a book in its hands. Scatter tons of leaves over the pile, in the tree, in the basket, and among the rakes. Tape leaves randomly to the tree. Place books in the basket and arrange leaves falling out.

TITLES:

> *Tree-mendous Fall Reading*
> *Fall for Tree-mendous Books*
> *Tree-mendous Historical Fiction*

BACKGROUND: Blue sky paper

BORDERS: None

LETTERINGS: Four-inch cutouts

PROPS: Tree (made on the opaque projector or a real tree limb); fall leaves; half-basket with books inside; corn husks; minicorns; artificial red apples and gourds

INSTRUCTIONS: Make a tree as tall as your bulletin board. Draw it freehand or use the opaque projector. Could choose to use a real tree limb. Staple it to the left side of the board. Staple the slogan to the middle of the board. Pin the basket in the bottom right corner. If a real basket is not available, make one on the opaque projector. Put books and apples in the basket. Staple leaves falling from the tree. Cover the ground with falling leaves. Staple minicorn, apples, and gourds against the basket. Real autumn leaves may be used if they are laminated first. Add other fall items as desired.

TITLES:

Tree-mendous Fall Reading
Tree-mendous Fall Books
Tree-mendous Books

BACKGROUND: Blue with clouds

BORDERS: None

FLOORING: Artificial turf painted autumn browns, golds, greens, red, etc.

LETTERINGS: Four-inch red cutouts

PROPS: Two tree branches (one on each side of showcase); autumn leaves; basket; ceramic pumpkins; artificial apples; corn husks; minicorn

INSTRUCTIONS: Staple background to walls of showcase. Put in flooring. Put one tree limb on left side and one on the right side of the showcase. Put basket in lower right corner. Put autumn leaves on tree and falling to the ground. Staple slogan to back wall of showcase toward the right. Put ceramic pumpkins, corn husks, minicorn, and artificial apples around basket. Place books with fall and autumn in the titles around the floor of the showcase. Scatter more autumn leaves around the books and basket.

TITLES:

Give Thanks for Books
Feast on Reading
Books Are Food for Thankful Thoughts

BACKGROUND: Dark blue sky or cloud sky background

BORDERS: Fall leaves (purchased) or small die-cut leaves

LETTERINGS: Black four-inch cutouts or pin backs

PROPS: Six small stuffed animals; red-and-white-checked napkin; Styrofoam stumps for chairs; autumn leaves; tree branch with autumn leaves; miniature books; brown acrylic paint; X-ACTO knife; Styrofoam block 10" x 2" or 3"

INSTRUCTIONS: Staple background and border to board. Fasten small tree limb to left side of board by stapling it or using a 10-inch piece of clear tape, which is centered and taped over the tree limb. The excess tape is stapled to the board. Cover tape and staples with autumn leaves. Repeat this technique in three spots. The smaller limbs may be stapled to the board to help stabilize the tree. Drape napkin over block like a tablecloth, then fasten the block and covering napkin horizontally to the board with T-pins. Paint stumps brown and cut them in half vertically. Fasten stumps with T-pins at each end of the table and two in front, over the cloth. Fasten animals to stumps as if they are seated around the table. Using tape, attach small books to the animals' paws. Scatter and staple leaves all over the ground and falling from the sky; arrange a few still on the tree.

TITLES:

Feast on Reading
Give Thanks for Books
Feast on Books
Have a Mind Feast . . . Read
Be Thankful for Books

BACKGROUND: Blue sky and cloud background

BORDERS: None

FLOORING: Artificial autumn-colored turf

LETTERINGS: Black cutouts or pin backs

PROPS: Tree limb; split-log table; six log stumps; assorted fall leaves; red-and-white-checked napkin or similar sized material; six or seven small stuffed animals; miniature books; limb of autumn leaves

INSTRUCTIONS: Staple background to walls of showcase. Put artificial turf on floor of showcase. Put tree limb in showcase on left side. Staple slogan to back wall of showcase. Place autumn leaves on tree limbs. Hang a limb of autumn leaves from ceiling of showcase and in the very front of top of showcase. Staple leaves randomly around slogan and on walls. Place the split log in the floor of the showcase. Place log stumps (two behind, two in front, and one on each end) around the table. Cover the table with the napkin tablecloth. Set small animal critters on stump chairs, and one under the tree. Attach small minibooks to their paws so they appear to be reading. Spread more autumn leaves everywhere.

TITLES:

Scout Native American History
Explore Native American Heritage
Discover Native American History

BACKGROUND: Brown wrapping paper or cork board

BORDERS: None

LETTERINGS: Hand-lettered on brown paper or light tan vinyl to look as if it is written on a piece of buckskin. Use black marker.

PROPS: Autumn leaves; ornamental corn and husks; vinyl or paper teepee; sticks for teepee poles; acrylic paints; markers; "Dream Catcher" (borrow, make, or buy one); war shield; brown paper canoe; baby moccasin; artifact-type cards with information about the dream catcher, war shield, canoes, and moccasins; other items of significance to Native Americans

INSTRUCTIONS: Staple background to the board. Staple the buckskin with the slogan in the center of the board. Make teepee, war shield, and canoe. Staple teepee, dream catcher, war shield, canoe, moccasin, and leaves to the bulletin board. Add the explanatory cards and legends by these artifacts. Staple autumn leaves, ornamental corn, and husks around all items and on background.

TITLES:

Scout Native American History
Explore Native American History
Discover Native American History

BACKGROUND: Brown wrapping paper or cork board

BORDERS: None

FLOORING: Artificial turf in autumn colors

LETTERINGS: Hand-lettered on brown paper or light tan vinyl to make it look as if it is written on a piece of buckskin (use black marker)

PROPS: Autumn leaves; breechclout; war shield; teepee made of tan vinyl or brown craft paper (enlarge pattern with opaque projector to a 28" radius); sticks for teepee poles; dream catcher; moccasin; canoe; Indian bead necklace; ornamental corn; ceramic pumpkins; small artifact-type cards explaining the significance of the featured items for Native Americans; books; branch of autumn leaves

INSTRUCTIONS: Staple background to the walls of the showcase. Place the autumn-colored artificial turf in the floor of the showcase. Center the buckskin with the slogan about one third from the top of the showcase. Hang the war shield from the top of the showcase or staple it to the back wall. Hang the breechclout in the upper left quadrant of the showcase. Hang the Indian bead necklace on the lower left wall. Put the teepee in the floor of the showcase on the right side of the showcase. Put the sticks for the teepee inside and coming out at the top. Stuff teepee with newspaper to hold its shape. Staple the dream catcher on the back wall. Put books, ceramic pumpkins, ornamental corn, and autumn leaves in the floor of the showcase. Place the moccasin and canoe in the foreground of the floor. Place cards explaining the significance of the items and their legends next to the item. Staple autumn leaves to the walls of the showcase. Scatter leaves around teepee and floor of showcase. Hang branch of autumn leaves in upper right quadrant of the showcase.

VARIATIONS: Use whatever Native American artifacts that are available.

TITLES:

Have a Cool Yule . . . Read!
Race into Yuletide Reading
Race into Reading

BACKGROUND: Dark blue and a white strip for paper ski slopes

BORDERS: None

LETTERINGS: White pin backs or four-inch cutouts

PROPS: Fake fur polar bear; candy cane skis (cut out of poster board and color with red markers); Santa hat, knit ski cap or stocking cap; black felt or paper nose and eyes; snowflakes; ski poles

INSTRUCTIONS: Staple blue background to board. Staple white paper ski slope in place. Make bear on poster board by enlarging the illustration of the bulletin board with an opaque projector. Use as a pattern to cut out white fake fur. Glue fur bear onto poster board for stiffening. Staple the bear to the board. Put Santa hat on the bear's head. Staple snowflakes on blue background. Make ski poles from metal wire or dowel rods. Attach ski poles to the bear and board with T-pins.

VARIATIONS: Could use cotton batting for ski slope to add more dimension and texture. Use blue wrapping paper with snowflakes for a different look. Switch hats to ski cap after the holidays and change to a generic winter slogan.

TITLES:

Skate into Reading
Have a Cool Yule . . . Read!
Skate to the Shelves and Read

BACKGROUND: Dark blue with scattered snowflakes or snowflake wrapping paper

BORDERS: None or blue with snowflakes (purchased)

FLOORING: Blue paper covered with waxed paper to make a frozen pond; surround with cotton-batting snow

LETTERINGS: Four-inch black cutouts or pin backs

PROPS: Three white stuffed bears; six real candy canes for ice skates; snowflakes; three knit hats for bears (Santa hats, ski hats, or stocking caps); books; cotton batting; wax paper frozen pond

INSTRUCTIONS: Staple background to the walls of the showcase. Attach slogan to back wall. Cover floor with blue paper, then waxed paper. Build up sides of floor to form base for cotton-batting snowdrifts. Surround edges of "frozen pond" with batting. Attach candy canes with rubber bands to bears' feet for skates. Put hats on bears. Seat the bears in the snow behind the pond, feet forward, and put books in their hands. Hang snowflakes from the ceiling and attach others to the inside of the glass with rubber cement.

VARIATIONS: May hang more winter-themed books with slings on side walls and place some around the bears in the snow.

TITLES:

Present the Gift of Reading
Give the Gift of Reading
Share the Gift of Reading

BACKGROUND: Red brick corrugated paper or colorful holiday wrapping paper

BORDERS: None

LETTERINGS: White, green cutouts or black pin backs

PROPS: Reindeer head made from opaque projector drawing; box wrapped as a gift with large bow; knit muffler

INSTRUCTIONS: Staple background to the bulletin board. Draw freehand or use the bulletin board illustration to make a reindeer head with the aid of the opaque projector. Attach reindeer to left bottom side and corner of the board. Wrap a muffler around its neck. Pin one end of the muffler in an upward position. Attach the slogan to the board. Use T-pins to attach the gift-wrapped box over the reindeer's hoof.

TITLES:

Present the Joy of Reading
Present the Gift of Reading
Share the Joy of Reading

BACKGROUND: White

BORDERS: None

FLOORING: Cotton batting for a snow blanket

LETTERINGS: Hand-lettered on round moon

PROPS: Small stuffed rabbits (substitute any animal); papier-mâché reindeer (substitute any animal); small pine tree; red bird; reading Santa (substitute any Santa doll or any doll to read to the woodland critters); books; gold moon; snowflakes (plastic); fishing line; cotton-batting snow blanket

INSTRUCTIONS: Staple background to walls of showcase. Build up bottom of showcase with books or wadded newspaper. Cover these mounds with cotton batting or white material. Trace the slogan on a large gold circle. Hang the gold circle with the slogan on it in the upper right quadrant. Place the pine tree in the lower left corner. Cover the trunk of the tree with the snow blanket. Place the reader (Santa, doll, or larger animal) in lower right corner. Put book in his hands. Place animals by the reader. Pose them so that they appear to be listening attentively to the story. Put a red bird or other birds and creatures around the scene as needed. Hang snowflakes on fishing line at different heights, or use rubber cement to place snowflakes on the glass.

TITLES:

Seasonal Readings
'Tis the Season to Be Reading
Holiday Reading

BACKGROUND: Green

BORDERS: Holly (purchased) or solid red

LETTERINGS: Four-inch red cutouts or white pin backs

PROPS: Large red velvet Santa bag; books; Styrofoam peppermint candy; red paint; crumpled newspaper; clear plastic wrap

INSTRUCTIONS: Staple background and borders to board. Staple slogan in the upper one-third of the board. Make a large Santa gift bag out of velvet or any red material or red paper. Fold material in half with right sides together. Stitch or hot glue down the two open sides. Turn the top down about four inches. Stitch or glue the top. Use a gold or red drawstring made from ribbon, robe cord, or any string. Cut a small hole in the side of the hem and string the drawstring through the casing with a safety pin. Turn the bag out with right side showing. Staple bag on the inside to the board. Stuff bag with newspapers. Put paperback books into top of bag. Fasten books to bulletin board with slings. Make peppermint candies from Styrofoam circles. Mark off triangles and paint or color with magic markers. Wrap plastic wrap around them. Pin them around the base of the bag and across the bottom of the board.

TITLES:

Seasonal Readings
'Tis the Season to Be Reading
Deck the Halls with Books and Holly

BACKGROUND: Red

BORDERS: None

FLOORING: None

LETTERINGS: Four-inch green cutouts or pin backs

PROPS: Two toy soldiers; tree ornaments; small decorated pine tree with tree skirt; snowflakes; two large wrapped rectangular boxes that are the same lengths but different widths; miniature books; pinecones; stacks of minibooks tied with ribbons

INSTRUCTIONS: Staple background to walls of showcase. Place and center the boxes in the showcase, the narrower one on top. These boxes then resemble steps. Staple slogan to the top of the showcase. Center the tree on the boxes. Put a toy soldier on each side of the tree and exactly the same distance from the tree. Place a stack of tied minibooks under the tree on each side. Place red ball decorations at the feet of the soldiers. On the bottom step place small open books or paperbacks. Place red tree ornaments between the books. Put pinecones and ornaments on the sides of the steps. Use rubber cement to stick snowflakes all over the side walls, back walls, and glass doors. Place pinecones on sides of boxes and anywhere needed to fill in blank spots and balance the board.

VARIATIONS: Substitute Santas, angels, animals, or other figures for toy soldiers.

TITLES:

Wrapped Up in Reading
Wrapped Up in Holiday Reading
Wrapped Up in Books

BACKGROUND: Red or green foil wrapping paper

BORDERS: None

LETTERINGS: Green cutouts or white pin backs

PROPS: Presents wrapped in contrasting and eye-appealing holiday wrapping paper; bows and ribbons; ribbon streamers; books; holiday sacks; green, red, and white tissue paper; small animals; miniature books; giant gift tag for a box

INSTRUCTIONS: Staple background to board. Staple letters as illustrated to the board. Place wrapped packages and gift bags in top left and bottom corners of the board. Place gift bags and smaller packages under the word *reading*. Put tissue paper in gift bags. Put small bears and animals peeking out of bags. Place miniature books in their paws. Add ribbon streamers where needed. Add extra bows. Put books under ribbons of wrapped packages. Make and place a giant gift tag that says, "Happy Holidays from the Media Center" in upper right corner of the board.

TITLES:

Wrapped Up in Reading
Wrapped Up in Holiday Books
Wrapped Up in Books

BACKGROUND: Red

BORDERS: None

FLOORING: Crumpled red, green, and white tissue paper

LETTERINGS: White pin backs or cutouts

PROPS: Large boxes covered in holiday wrapping paper; lids covered separately with large bows on them; two stuffed animals; tissue paper; decorated tree limb; tree ornaments; books; miniature books; giant gift tag for box

INSTRUCTIONS: Wrap different sized boxes. Wrap lids separately. Leave lids off the boxes. Hang decorated tree branch across top of showcase. Staple slogan in middle left of board. Put tissue paper in boxes. Put stuffed animals in boxes. Add books to stuffed animals' paws for them to read. Leave lids off boxes, but hanging on boxes. Attach the large gift tag to the front of the box on right side. The tag reads, "Happy Holidays from the Library." Scrunch tissue paper and place all over the floor of the showcase. Add books, ornaments, and miniature books to the tissue paper arrangement.

TITLES:

Believe!
Read About the Many Faces of Santa
I Believe!

BACKGROUND: Red

BORDERS: Holly border (purchased) or artificial holly garland

LETTERINGS: Large white pin backs or cutouts

PROPS: Pictures of Santa Claus through the years, old versions, modern ones, other cultures; a copy of *Yes, Virginia, There Is a Santa Claus*

INSTRUCTIONS: Staple the background to the board. Could use wrapping paper. Staple the page with *Yes, Virginia* in the center of the bulletin board. Use white pin-backed letters that spell "Believe . . ." above *Yes, Virginia* page. Pin up the other pictures of Santa in a collage effect or magazine graphic layout look.

TITLES:

Believe!
The Many Personas of Santa
Do You Believe?

BACKGROUND: Green

BORDERS: Holly (purchased) or any holiday border

FLOORING: Green continued from the walls

LETTERINGS: Four-inch red cutouts

PROPS: As many Santas as can be borrowed or collected; pictures of different versions of Santas; stacks of holiday books; Santa ornaments; copy of *Yes, Virginia, There Is a Santa Claus*

INSTRUCTIONS: Put a strip of the green background paper across the floor. Staple background and border to the walls of the showcase. Staple slogan to the center of the wall. Staple *Yes, Virginia* under the slogan. Arrange larger Santas in the back of the showcase, then add the remaining ones. Put stacks of holiday books in the floor and around the Santas. Use T-pins to hang Santa ornaments on the side walls and background where needed.

TITLES:

Read in the New Year
Ring in the New Year
New Year of Reading

BACKGROUND: Winter wrapping paper or royal blue with white strip of batting for snowdrifts

BORDERS: Snowflake border (purchased) or solid blue

LETTERINGS: White pin backs or cutouts

PROPS: Cotton batting for snow drifts; black top hat; stuffed polar bear or make one from poster board or white fake fur; New Year's party hats and streamers; red paper banner with white pin back letters (staple through letter and banners onto board); paper or plastic snowflakes; red muffler for bear

INSTRUCTIONS: Staple background and border to board. Staple cotton batting at the bottom for snowdrifts. Cut the banner out of red wrapping or craft paper in the shape of a muffler with fringed ends. Make a polar bear out of poster board, white fake fur, or use a stuffed bear. Put a real muffler around its neck. Use a black top hat or make one from black construction paper. Fasten the bear in the right corner with T-pins so that it looks as if it is sitting in the snow. Fasten a book to the board with a sling to look as if the bear is reading it. Staple New Year's party hats, streamers, and blowers to the board. Staple the banner in the center of the board. Use white pin-backed letters to pin the slogan on the banner. Staple snowflakes across the background as needed. If white background was used, place die-cut blue snowflakes on the background.

TITLES:

Read in the New Year
Resolve to READ in the New Year
Books to Read in the New Year

BACKGROUND: Winter wrapping paper or royal blue

BORDERS: None

FLOORING: White batting for snowdrifts

LETTERINGS: White pin backs or four-inch cutouts

PROPS: Cotton batting for snowdrifts; black top hat; white stuffed polar bear; New Year's party hats and streamers; red paper banner; bottled water; books; snowflakes; red muffler for bear

INSTRUCTIONS: Staple background to the showcase walls. Make the banner the width of the back wall of the showcase. Laminate it; then fringe the ends with scissors. Use white pin-backed letters to spell out the slogan. Build up the showcase floor with newspaper and books. Cover these mounds with cotton batting to create snowdrifts. Put a muffler around the bear's neck and a black top hat on his head. Place the party hats and streamers in the corners and against the walls. Scatter blowers, streamers, and bottled water on the floor. Place books around these items. Hang snowflakes from ceiling of showcase at various heights to fill in blank spots. Do not cover slogan with snowflakes. Use rubber cement to place snowflakes around walls and glass of showcase.

TITLES:

Winter Brings Good Knights to Read
In Days of Old When Knights Were Cold . . . They Read!
In Days of Old When Knights Were Bold

BACKGROUND: Fancy gold-patterned wrapping paper or gold-flocked wallpaper

BORDERS: Gold

LETTERINGS: White pin backs

PROPS: Small knights made from poster board, computer graphics, or purchase; heraldry shields; pictures of suits of armor; whatever can be collected about knights; books or a list of books about knights and castles

INSTRUCTIONS: Staple background and border to the board. Put up slogan across upper one-third of board. Pin collected knights, heraldry shields, castle pieces, and pictures around the slogan. Add books by using slings.

VARIATIONS: Add pictures of castles, or poster of castles or knights. Could use poster board knight chess pieces made with aid of the opaque projector.

TITLES:

Winter Brings Good Knights to Read
Winter Knights Bring Time to Read
Read the Winter Knights Away

BACKGROUND: Elegant gold-patterned wrapping or wallpaper

BORDERS: None

FLOORING: Off-white satin

LETTERINGS: White pin backs or four-inch cutouts

PROPS: Knight statues; models or opaque projector-created stand-ups of heraldry shields; pictures of suits of armor and other medieval times items; books about knights and castles; gold antique-looking books; heraldry shields

INSTRUCTIONS: Staple background to walls of showcase. Staple slogan to back wall of showcase. Drape and arrange the off-white fabric in the floor of showcase. Hang knights on walls of showcase by making a sling of string, twine, or ribbon thumbtacked to board, around chest, and under arms. Place the larger knights in the corner of the showcase. Add more knights (if available) in the floor of the showcase. Place books in the floor of the showcase in front of and beside knights. Place books in the arms of knights, if possible.

TITLES:

Snow Time Is Book Time
Warm Up with Reading
Bundle Up with Books

BACKGROUND: Blue with white strip of snowdrifts

BORDERS: Snowflakes (purchased or die cuts)

LETTERINGS: White pin backs or cutouts

PROPS: Snowman (either poster board of enlarged picture done on white paper with aid of opaque projector, or cotton batting) cutout; toy broom; muffler and mittens; black top hat (poster board or stiff paper); white paper or cotton-batting snowdrifts; snowflakes; paperback book

INSTRUCTIONS: Staple background and border to the board. Staple paper or cotton-batting snowdrifts across the bottom of the board. Put slogan up on right side of the board. Make snowman with aid of opaque projector and the bulletin board illustration. Make arms from same material as snowman. Put muffler around the neck, mittens on the hands. Fasten snowman and his arms firmly to the bulletin board. Put black top hat on the snowman. Fasten paperback winter-themed book to snowman by tacking strips of poster board across the bottom corners, then staple or pin arms over the books so that it looks as if the hands are holding it. Tuck the broom in one arm and secure by a strip thumbtacked around the handle, just under the straw. Book can be changed often (example: Use *A Christmas Carol* for the weeks before the holidays; then change to a book with a winter theme when you return in January and leave it there until you have time to change the entire board.) Staple snowflakes around the board as needed for balance.

TITLES:

Snow Time Is Book Time
Snow-Time Reading
Warm Up with Reading

BACKGROUND: Blue

BORDERS: None

FLOORINGS: Cotton batting for snow

LETTERINGS: White pin backs or cutouts

PROPS: Twigs for arms of snowman; red birds; tree limb; books; top hat; muffler; snowflakes; snowman; animals

INSTRUCTIONS: Staple background to walls of showcase. Build up the floor of the showcase with books and wadded-up newspaper. Cover the lumps with white cotton batting. Put the slogan on the back wall of the showcase. Create a snowman made from white garbage bags or purchase one at a craft store. Stuff a large white garbage bag with old white clothes, or triple-layer the bags and stuff with newspapers. Stuff one-third of the bag, then use a white twisty tie to gather it up. Stuff next section of bag, then tie it off, and stuff last third of bag and tie it off. Mold head so that eyes, nose, and mouth can be drawn on. Hot glue or tape twigs to snowman for arms. Put tree limb in the showcase on the left side. Place the snowman in the middle of the showcase. Put hat on the snowman's head and a muffler on his neck. Place a book in the twig arms of the snowman. Staple the slogan above the snowman's head. Place a red bird and animals around the snowman. Hang snowflakes from the ceiling. Add books about snow and winter to the snowbanks.

TITLES:

> *Winterize with Reading*
> *Winterize with Books*
> *Winterize with These Auto Reads*

BACKGROUND: Blue background, cotton batting for snowbanks in foreground

BORDERS: Snowflake border (purchased)

LETTERINGS: Four-inch white cutouts

PROPS: Books about car repairs, automobiles, auto mechanics; snowflakes

INSTRUCTIONS: Staple background to board. Staple cotton batting to bottom of board to resemble snowbanks. Staple slogan to board as illustrated. Attach books about cars and repairs to the board by using slings. Randomly staple snowflakes to board where needed.

TITLES:

Winterize with Reading
Winterize with Books
You "Auto" Winterize with Books

BACKGROUND: White with red brick corrugated paper on the bottom one-fourth of showcase to give the appearance of a brick wall

BORDERS: None

FLOORING: White cotton batting

LETTERING: Four-inch blue cutouts

PROPS: Snowflakes (blue die cut and large white plastic ones); pine tree; large toy car or jeep; books; cotton batting; two 10-inch fashion dolls (male and female)

INSTRUCTIONS: Staple background to walls of showcase. Staple slogan as illustrated. Build up bottom of showcase with boxes. Cover the boxes with cotton batting to give the appearance of snowy ground. Put the pine tree in the left corner. Stack books about cars and auto repairs in the floor of the showcase. Put the toy car or jeep in the showcase with its front end resting on the books. Place books by the pine tree, behind the car, and on the right side of showcase. Set the female doll dressed in winter clothes on top of books in the right corner. Place the male doll lying under the car and working on it. Place cotton batting along edges of the wall, on tree, and on books. Use a die-cutting machine to cut out blue snowflakes. Staple blue snowflakes to walls of showcase. Hang large white snowflakes from the top of showcase with fishing line. Rubber cement more blue snowflakes to inside of glass as needed.

VARIATIONS: Use several male dolls working on the jeep or use several female dolls working on the jeep.

TITLES:

Oldies But Goodies
Rockin' n Rollin' n Readin'
Reading Fifties-Style (or Sixties, Seventies)

BACKGROUND: Gold wrapping paper

BORDERS: Black music notes (purchased) or die cuts taped together in strips in the correct lengths and laminated

LETTERINGS: Black four-inch cutouts

PROPS: Old records (45's and 78's); round circles with titles, authors, and call numbers written on them to be rubber cemented over existing labels

INSTRUCTIONS: Staple background and border to board. Staple slogan to border. Make round labels to replace existing labels on old records. Write titles, authors, and call numbers on the labels. Pin records to the board with pushpins through the center hole.

TITLES:

Oldies But Goodies
The Reading Beat Goes On
Golden Oldies

BACKGROUND: Red or gold

BORDERS: None

FLOORING: None or wood

LETTERINGS: Black four-inch cutouts

PROPS: Books (favorites and classics); old 45 or 78 records (can find at thrift store, garage sales, or school AV rooms); party streamers; music notes; pushpins; miniature jukebox (or buy a large jukebox cutout at party supply store); small dolls in fifties-style clothes; circles for book titles to be rubber cemented over record labels

INSTRUCTIONS: Staple background to walls of showcase. Staple slogan to center of back wall. Print book titles on circles and rubber cement them onto the record labels. Surround slogan with records pinned to walls with pushpins. Hang party streamers from ceiling and walls of the showcase. Arrange stacks of old favorites and classic books in floor and corners of the showcase. Place miniature jukebox in center of showcase. Place dolls by books and even on books. Hang more records from ceiling of showcase with fishing line. Use rubber cement to stick music notes to walls and glass of the showcase. Add other memorabilia as desired.

VARIATIONS: Buy jukebox posters and cutouts from party supply stores if a miniature jukebox is not available. Use toy or model cars from the fifties and sixties among the books.

TITLES:

Sweetheart Reading
Books Are Real Treats
Love Your Books

BACKGROUND: Red

BORDERS: Hearts (purchased)

LETTERINGS: White pin backs

PROPS: Large empty heart-shaped candy box; large muffin paper cups; flat sheet of Styrofoam or foam core board to use to cut out hearts approximately five inches in diameter; pastel acrylic paints; red Sharpie fine point marker

INSTRUCTIONS: Staple background to the board. Staple border around the edges. Fasten the bottom half of the candy box in the upper left corner, hanging slightly over the edge. Attach the slogan as illustrated. Attach lid with tape in a slightly open position. Make hearts by cutting them out of the Styrofoam sheet or foam core board with an X-ACTO knife. Paint the hearts with several different pastel colors. When the hearts are fully dry, write titles of romantic books on them with the Sharpie pen. Put hearts in muffin cups and pin them to the board so they appear to be falling out of the candy box.

VARIATIONS: Cut out construction paper hearts in place of Styrofoam ones. Glue hearts to small pieces of Styrofoam and put them into the cups. Could just pin the Styrofoam heart candy around the box and find miniature book covers. Glue these small books to Styrofoam and pin them to the board through the muffin cups.

TITLES:

Read to Your Sweetheart
Cuddle Up and Read
Read with Your Honey

BACKGROUND: Red-with-white-hearts wrapping paper

BORDERS: None

FLOORING: Green burlap or artificial green turf

LETTERINGS: Four-inch black cutouts

PROPS: Monkeys and gorillas (any collection of animals or even a variety of different animals would work); books; leafy vines; branches of artificial green plants; green burlap or green material; Spanish moss

INSTRUCTIONS: Staple background to showcase walls. Build up floor of showcase with newspapers and books to make several mounds and lumps. Cover the mounds and hills with green burlap. Staple slogan to back walls of board. Hang vines from both sides and across the top of showcase. Hang clumps of Spanish moss streaming from vines. Place animals in a set of two, a group of three, and even one hanging from the vines at the top. Pose them so they look as if they are good listeners and readers. Place books in their "hands." Choose books about their species and families, or make them all romance books. Scatter Spanish moss around the books, burlap, and animals.

TITLES:

Un BULL ievable Books
Books are Un BULL ievable
BE BULL ievable . . . Research the Facts

BACKGROUND: Red

BORDERS: Black

LETTERINGS: Red pin backs or cutouts

PROPS: Picture of a bull; mini-basketball goal; small basketball; basketball books

INSTRUCTIONS: Staple background, then the border to the board. Use T-pins to pin a mini-basketball goal and small basketball to the board. Attach the slogan with the bull picture approximately one-fourth from the top of the board. Use slings to hang colorful basketball books.

TITLES:

Un BULL ievable Books
Un BULL ievable Reading
Be BULL ievable . . . Read!

BACKGROUND: Red

BORDERS: None

FLOORING: None, leave hardwood floor

LETTERINGS: Four-inch black cut-outs or pin backs

PROPS: Chicago Bulls towel; miniature basketball goal; Michael Jordan doll (substitute posters, cutouts from posters of NBA Stars, a full-sized basketball, basketball shoes, old school basketball uniforms, team pennants, and other items as needed); basketball and sports biographies

INSTRUCTIONS: Staple background to walls of showcase. Staple slogan to back wall. Place the basketball goal in upper left corner. Drape and pin towel in lower left two-thirds of showcase. Place doll in right bottom corner. Arrange basketball and sports biographies in front of draped towel and on floor in various positions. Put one or two paperbacks or miniature books in the goal. Tape net together so that the book does not fall through.

TITLES:

Tool Time Is Reading Time
Books Are Tools for the Future
Books Build Dreams

BACKGROUND: Blue or orange

BORDERS: Yardsticks or rulers

LETTERINGS: Black cutouts or pin backs

PROPS: Large plastic toy tools; wrench; hammer; screwdriver; black paper nail; balsa wood scraps; books on carpentry, construction, architecture, and woodworking; white paper screws

INSTRUCTIONS: Fasten background to the board. Tape yardsticks around the edges of the board, letting them protrude on the short sides and be short on the long sides. Fasten slogan to board. Arrange book covers or paper book shapes in the shape of a house. Use black half-inch paper strips to outline the shape of the house. Pin, tape, or use slings to attach books to board and toy tools around the house.

TITLES:

Tool Time Is Reading Time
Build Your Research Skills
Build Your Dreams

BACKGROUND: Drafting paper, blueprints, graph paper, or solid blue paper

BORDERS: Rulers or yardsticks

FLOORING: Sandpaper, wood shavings, excelsior shavings, or Spanish moss

LETTERINGS: Black pin backs, cutouts, or wood letters

PROPS: Toy or real hammers, screwdrivers, saw, nails, wrench, wood scraps, and sandpaper; books about woodworking and home building and magazines on the same topics; handsaw

INSTRUCTIONS: Staple background paper to walls. Pin rulers or yardsticks to outside edges with pushpins or tacks. Staple slogan to back of showcase wall. Secure toy or real tools around the slogan using T-pins or by tying fishing line around them and then wrapping the line around the pushpins or hanging them from the ceiling with fishing line. Put sandpaper or wood shavings over floor of showcase. Use scrap wood to make a display of partially constructed frame for box or birdhouse. Put the birdhouse and books on the bottom left side. Place a handsaw on the floor in the bottom right corner. Arrange woodworking books and magazines around the showcase floor. Hang books on the walls by using slings.

VARIATIONS: Wood letter shapes could be scattered around the books.

TITLES:

Heartbreakers and Tearjerkers
Heartbreaking Books
Broken-Hearted Reading

BACKGROUND: White

BORDERS: Hearts (purchased or use die cuts)

LETTERINGS: Four-inch red cutouts

PROPS: Six broken hearts (cut down the middle with jagged edges); titles of sad and tragic books; foam core poster board or Styrofoam sheet (half-inch); permanent marker or black or white paint pen

INSTRUCTIONS: Staple background to showcase. Staple border at the edges. Staple slogan in the middle of the board. Use foam core poster board or a sheet of one-half-inch Styrofoam to make broken hearts. Trace the heart shape (approximately six-inch hearts) onto the foam core or Styrofoam. Cut out hearts. Cut each heart down the middle with jagged cuts. Write book titles on the hearts with a permanent magic marker or a white paint pen. Staple or pin hearts around the slogan.

TITLES:

The Love of Reading Is Not Gone with the Wind
Romantic Historical Reading
Historical Fiction Is Not Gone with the Wind

BACKGROUND: Mural of Tara at sunset with a landscaped lawn made with the aid of the opaque projector, or use a solid coordinating color

BORDERS: None

FLOORING: Green burlap or artificial turf

LETTERINGS: Four-inch white cutouts and smaller pin backs for the first part of slogan

PROPS: *Gone with the Wind* dolls (substitute any dolls dressed in Civil War uniforms or civilian costumes for that time); could use *Gone with the Wind* posters, scenes, or characters made by using the opaque projector; Spanish moss; books of historical fiction; green burlap or artificial turf; small flowers

INSTRUCTIONS: Make a mural of Tara with aid of the opaque projector. Staple it to the walls of the showcase. Staple the slogan in the top one-third of the showcase. Crumple newspaper and place in the showcase floor to make small hills. Cover these hills with green burlap or artificial turf. Place the dolls in the front of the showcase. Place a copy of *Gone with the Wind* by the dolls. Add more historical fiction to the bottom of the showcase unless the option to feature only *Gone with the Wind* is chosen. Pin Spanish moss to the trees in the mural to complete the look of the Old South and a three-dimensional effect. Place small flowers in the green burlap.

VARIATIONS: If *Gone with the Wind* dolls are not an option, create a generic historical fiction showcase with farms, wagons, horses, and other historical items. A three-dimensional puzzle of Tara has been released to retail stores; this puzzle of Tara would go well with this showcase, but use a solid background.

TITLES:

Devoted Dog Tales
Hopelessly Devoted to You
Doggy Tales

BACKGROUND: White

BORDERS: "Scottie" border (purchased), dog border, heart border, or solid red border

LETTERINGS: Black cutouts or pin backs

PROPS: Computer printed book titles; red hearts; Scottie dog cut out of black fake fur; three-inch-wide red ribbon one yard long

INSTRUCTIONS: Use the opaque projector to make the Scottie dog out of fake fur. Use illustration on this page to make a Scottie on the overhead projector. Tape one-half yard of black fake fur on the wall with the furry side to the wall. Place pattern in the opaque projector. Project the pattern onto material to the desired size. The one used in the model is approximately 24 inches long and 15 inches high. Use a white paint pen or black Sharpie pen to trace the pattern. The white pen will be easier to see, but black can also work. Cut out pattern. To preserve the dog prop over a long term, stitch around edges by hand or machine to keep edges of material from unraveling. Staple background to the board. Staple slogan across the top. Staple the Scottie to the bulletin board. Staple hearts around the dog. Tie ribbon around neck of dog. Make a large bow. Arrange titles over hearts around the dog. (Even high school seniors stop to "pet" this display!)

TITLES:

Devoted Dog Tales
Dog Tales
Tales of Dog Devotion

BACKGROUND: Blue cloud background

BORDERS: None

FLOORING: Artificial green turf and other green grass

LETTERINGS: Black cutouts or pin backs

PROPS: Books; Scottie dog cut out of black fake fur or stuffed toy dogs; white picket fence; red hearts; red flowering bushes; green artificial grass; three-inch wide red ribbon approximately one yard in length

INSTRUCTIONS: Staple background to walls of the showcase. Staple slogan to back wall. Place the green artificial turf in the floor of the showcase. Make the Scottie on the preceding bulletin board page. Staple the Scottie to cardboard, heavy poster board, or foam core board. Cut out the shape of the Scottie. Tie ribbon around his neck into a big bow. Place the fence against the showcase wall. Put red flowering bushes behind the fence. Place the Scottie in the middle of the showcase. Put a block of wood, bricks, or books behind his feet to keep him standing. Place a book at each foot to keep him from falling forward. Hang books on side walls with slings. Place other books in the grass. Spread other artificial grass (such as excelsior wood grass) around books, fence, and dog. Staple hearts around slogan.

TITLES:

These Books "Quack" Me Up!
Books "Quack" Me Up
These Books Are Real "Quack-Ups"

BACKGROUND: Blue cloud and grass strip for bottom

BORDERS: None

LETTERINGS: White pin backs or cutouts

PROPS: Three ducks walking; three yards of ribbon; books; white fence (plastic); flowers

INSTRUCTIONS: Staple background to board. Staple slogan to the board. Staple grass strip to bottom of board. Make ducks with aid of illustration on this page and the opaque projector. Laminate and staple the ducks to the board. Tie the ribbon in a continuous line on each duck by starting at one end or the other. Pin the ends to the board as if it is blowing in the wind. Attach white fence in front of the ducks and grass. Write titles of humorous books on blades of grass.

VARIATIONS: Put cotton batting on the clouds, or if solid blue is used, make clouds of cotton batting and use rubber cement to attach them to the laminated background. Hang humorous books to the board by using slings or hang a humorous book list to the board on the top side of the slogan.

TITLES:

These Books "Quack" Me Up
Books to "Quack" You Up
Books Are Real "Quack-Ups"

BACKGROUND: Light blue with clouds

BORDERS: None

FLOORING: Green indoor-outdoor carpeting

LETTERINGS: Four-inch white cutouts or pin backs

PROPS: Plastic mother duck; baby ducks; white plastic fence; flowers; books; make miniature fake books for the little ducks to read

INSTRUCTIONS: Staple background to showcase walls. Staple slogan to back wall. Build up the showcase floor with books and boxes. Cover them with artificial grass turf. Put the plastic fence towards the back of the showcase. Put flowers behind the fence to create a flower bed. Place the mother duck in front of the fence and to the left side of the showcase. Place all the little ducks in a row behind mom. Can use any little ducks available (rubber duckies, baby toys, etc.). Ducks do not have to match. Put a humorous book (such as Art Linkletter's *Kids Say the Darndest Things*) propped open in front of mom. Make books for babies by folding card stock or index cards and writing titles of funny books from the library catalog. Pictures from old vendor catalogs could be cut out and glued onto these cards to make them look like real minibooks. Scatter small flowers in and around the ducks.

TITLES:

Explore the Sci-Fi Galaxy
"Take Us to Your Readers"
Blast Off with a Good Book

BACKGROUND: Black garbage bags or paper

BORDERS: None

LETTERINGS: Aluminum foil cutouts (laminate the aluminum foil before cutting out letters)

PROPS: UFO's made from six pie pans; sci-fi titles; aluminum foil stars

INSTRUCTIONS: Staple background to board. Center slogan and staple. Make six UFOs out of six aluminum pie pans. Fold the pie pan in half. Crimp the edges together with pliers. Pie pans from graham cracker crusts work best because they have an edge that is easy to crimp. Tape names of sci-fi titles to the top of the UFO. Use T-pins to attach the top back portion through the pan and into the board. Also T-pins or straight pins could be pushed to the left and right edges of the UFOs to make them stay up better. Staple silver foil stars around the board where needed.

VARIATIONS: Could leave pie pans partially open and rubber cement little green men made out of green chenille sticks. These "men" could be stick figures or bought aliens used in a shadow-box effect.

TITLES:

Explore the Sci-Fi Galaxy
Star Fiction
Space: The Final Frontier

BACKGROUND: Black garbage bags

BORDERS: None

FLOORING: Black garbage bags

LETTERINGS: Red pin backs or four-inch red cutouts

PROPS: *Star Wars* and *Star Trek* memorabilia; moons and planets; black garbage bags; books; three-inch foil stars in gold and silver

INSTRUCTIONS: Staple background to walls of the showcase. Build up showcase walls with old books on either side. Put only a few books in the middle so that it is noticeably lower than the two sides. Cover these books with black garbage bags. Place different memorabilia around and on these created mountains and valleys as illustrated. Staple slogan to back wall. Arrange *Star Wars* and *Star Trek* books around and on the memorabilia. Use rubber cement to stick gold and silver stars to the background and to the glass doors of the showcase.

VARIATIONS: Hang spaceship models and UFOs from the ceiling of the showcase. Could also hang models of planets instead of using flat pictures of them. Often, these models of planets can be borrowed from the science department.

TITLES:

Swing into Spring Reading
Swing into Spring with Good Books
Swing into Sports Reading

BACKGROUND: Yellow

BORDERS: Rainbow (purchased) or solid pink or red

LETTERINGS: Four-inch red cutouts or red pin backs

PROPS: Tennis racquet; racquetball racquet; badminton racquet; toy plastic baseball bat; toy or real golf club; cardboard or Styrofoam balls with sports titles written on them

INSTRUCTIONS: Staple background to the board. Then staple the border to the edges of the board. Center and staple slogan to the board. Attach the racquets, golf club, and bat strategically around the slogan. Make baseballs, softballs, golf balls, tennis balls, and badminton shuttlecocks out of cardboard or Styrofoam balls of different sizes. Write sports titles on them with a Sharpie and pin them around the racquets as needed.

TITLES:

Swing into Spring Reading
Swing into Sports Books
Swing into the Library for a Good Book

BACKGROUND: Cloud background or light blue

BORDERS: None

FLOORING: Green artificial turf

LETTERINGS: Four-inch green cutouts

PROPS: Racquets (tennis, racquetball, badminton; substitute any other kind of racquets, real or toy); golf clubs; baseball bat; balls (tennis, golf, Ping-Pong, baseball); shuttlecock; books on swinging sports

INSTRUCTIONS: Staple background to the showcase walls. Build up the showcase floor with boxes. Cover them with green artificial turf. Lean bat and badminton racquet in left corner of showcase. Hang racquetball racquet with fishing line on left side of showcase. Hang golf club in top right quadrant of showcase. Hang another racquet with fishing line from top of right side of showcase. Arrange books in the floor of the showcase. Highlight books using different types of balls in the showcase floor. Lay a golf club in the floor of the showcase in front of balls and books.

TITLES:

Spring into Reading
Spring into Action . . . Read!
Spring Fever Reading

BACKGROUND: Yellow or wrapping paper with small flowers

BORDERS: Flowers (purchased) or single artificial flowers like tulips or jonquils twisted together to make the appropriate lengths for a border around the four sides

LETTERINGS: Four-inch green or red pin backs

PROPS: Plastic slinkies or chenille craft sticks or a mixture of the two (could substitute any other available types of springs); single flowers to match border; list of books with *spring* in the title

INSTRUCTIONS: Staple background to the bulletin board. Staple border onto the edges. Staple or pin the slogan in the middle of upper third of the board. Staple or secure with T-pins one end of slinkies to the board. Let the rest of the slinkie fall forward to create a spring effect. Wrap chenille craft strips around a magic marker. Staple or secure with T-pins one end of the chenille craft strip to the board; then gently stretch it to give the appearance of a spring. Staple the list of books with *spring* in the titles in the center of the board. Staple flowers around the edges of the list. Staple single flowers strategically around the board. Make and staple as many springs as needed to balance the arrangement.

TITLES:

Spring Fever Reading
Spring into Reading
Spring into Books

BACKGROUND: Blue with clouds

BORDERS: None

FLOORING: Green artificial turf

LETTERINGS: Four-inch green cutouts

PROPS: White fence; flowers; doll; small quilt; books; bugs; ants; tree limb; green leaves or leafy vines

INSTRUCTIONS: Staple background to showcase walls. Build up floor with boxes. Cover boxes with green artificial turf. Place fence crossways in the left corner. Put tree limb behind fence. Add spring green leaves to the tree. Arrange flower bushes around the base of the tree and behind the fence. Staple slogan to the back showcase wall. Spread small quilt or blanket (baby or doll-sized) on the right side of showcase grass. Stack up books with *spring* in the titles (about 10 books tall) in the middle of the showcase and on the far right corner of the quilt. Pose small doll sitting on quilt and leaning against the stack of books . Put book in doll's hands. Letter the title *Symptoms of Spring Fever* onto the book the doll is reading. Scatter small flowers around. Put ants and other small bugs on grass in floor.

TITLES:

De Bug Your Brain . . . Read!
Buggy About Books
Don't Bug Us! Read!

BACKGROUND: Yellow

BORDERS: None

LETTERINGS: Red four-inch cutouts

PROPS: Green strip of grass cut from craft paper; three large ladybugs (purchased or made from Styrofoam); red, black, and blue paint

INSTRUCTIONS: Staple background to the board. Staple grass strip across the bottom of the board, allowing some blades to overlap the bottom bugs. Staple slogan across the board as illustrated. Purchased ladybugs are fastened by stretching a rubber band over the two front legs and two back legs from the underneath side of the bug. It will look like a square of rubber band around the bug's abdomen. Place a T-pin in the board at the desired location and hook the two sides of the square around the pin. If bugs are not available, make them. Buy two large Styrofoam balls. Cut them in half. Paint them red and let them dry. When they are dry, paint black ovals on the red half circles. Paint solid black about two inches from the edge of the ball. Paint blue eyes. Cut black chenille sticks in lengths of three inches and five inches. Stick the three-inch length into the head of the bug for antennae. Stick the five-inch chenille craft sticks into the sides of the bugs (three on each side) to make them look like legs. Use T-pins to stick the bugs to the board.

VARIATIONS: Make minibooks for the bugs to read. Use smaller Styrofoam balls and make approximately 12 to 16 ladybugs. The smaller bugs are also quite eye-catching.

TITLES:

De Bug Your Brain . . . Read! (feature
computer books)
Buggy About Books
Books That Drive Us Buggy! (feature
insect books)

BACKGROUND: Yellow or cloud paper

BORDERS: None

FLOORING: Artificial turf grass with
green craft paper strip across base.

LETTERINGS: Red four-inch cutouts

PROPS: Three to six ladybugs (if smaller
bugs are used, then use more. Could make
bugs from Styrofoam following instructions
on preceding bulletin board page); rocks;
spring flowers; artificial blades of grass; tree
limb; logs; green leaves; books

INSTRUCTIONS: Staple background to
showcase walls. Put in flooring. Could make mounds first from crumpled newspapers if so desired.
Cover with artificial turf or green burlap. Put tree and rocks into showcase. Staple slogan in the
center of the board. Place bugs on rocks, logs, in the tree, and in the grass. Place books about
computers strategically around the floor of the showcase. Put spring flowers around to complete
the effect. Use slings to attach books to side walls of the showcase as needed. Attach green leaves
to increase the springtime look.

VARIATIONS: Use all kinds of bugs, grasshoppers, and beanie-baby bugs.

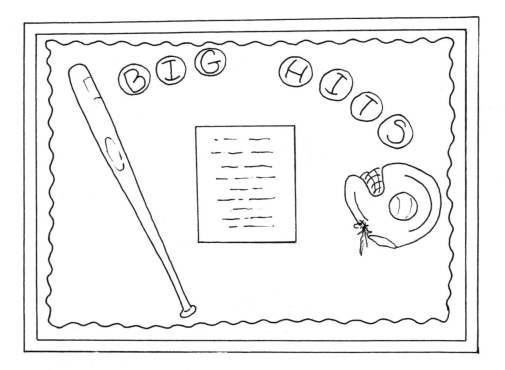

TITLES:

Big Hits
Books Are Big Hits
Read a Big Hit

BACKGROUND: Red

BORDERS: Ball border (purchased) or solid blue

LETTERINGS: Styrofoam balls

PROPS: Baseball glove; Styrofoam balls; plastic baseball bat; computer list of baseball books

INSTRUCTIONS: Staple background and border to board. Attach plastic bat on the left side of the board. Attach the baseball glove on the right side of the board. Make Styrofoam balls that spell out "Big Hits" according to instructions on following showcase page. Attach balls to the board, placing them in an arc. Staple the list of books to the middle of the board.

TITLES:

Big Hits
Books Are Big Hits
Sports Books Are Big Hits

BACKGROUND: Cloud paper or solid blue

BORDERS: None

FLOORING: Sandpaper or brown paper

LETTERINGS: Styrofoam balls

PROPS: Styrofoam balls approximately the size of baseballs; batter (doll or stand-up made with the opaque projector or cut from a sports poster of a sports figure batting. Use rubber cement to attach to foam core poster board); pitcher (doll or stand-up made with the aid of the opaque projector; books; home plate made from construction paper

INSTRUCTIONS: Staple background to the walls of the showcase. Place the sandpaper in the floor of the showcase so that it looks like dirt. Buy four Styrofoam balls. Cut the balls in half. Use a red permanent marker to draw two lines on the ball (look at a real baseball to emulate these lines). Put slash marks by these lines to resemble the stitching. Use a magic marker and write one letter in the middle of each half-ball: B I G H I T S. Use the opaque projector to make players, buy a poster of a sports figure, or use dolls to simulate a pitcher and batter. If the poster option is used, cut out the baseball player. Rubber cement player to a piece of foam core poster board. Then prop player in the corner of the showcase. Put a fake home plate in front of cutout. Try to stand up the dolls or the opaque projector-created players (leaning them against the showcase side walls helps stabilize them). Pin through the dolls and into the showcase wall to keep them in place. Place the batter on the left and the pitcher on the right. Make a home plate out of construction paper and place it in front of the batter. Place the Styrofoam balls on the back wall of the showcase in an arc from the pitcher to the batter. Have baseball books standing up between the two players. Lay other baseball books on the floor to enhance the overall effect.

TITLES:

Stormy Weather Reading
Storm Time Is Time to Read Weather Tips
Storm Time Is Weather Safety-Tip Reading Time

BACKGROUND: Navy blue

BORDERS: None

LETTERINGS: Aluminum foil four-inch cutouts (laminate foil before cutting out letters)

PROPS: Three twisters made from quilt batting; lightning bolts; aluminum foil raindrops; small twigs; black acrylic craft paint

INSTRUCTIONS: Staple background to board. Center slogan on board. Make three twisters by taking coat hangers apart. Twist wire into a spiral, getting smallest spiral at the bottom. Wrap cotton batting around the wire. Dab black paint randomly over batting. Pin twisters to board with T-pins or staples. Stick pieces of twigs out of the twister. Staple or rubber cement book titles to top of twisters. Make lightning bolts out of poster board or cardboard. Cover the bolts with aluminum foil and laminate. Use rubber cement to stick foil raindrops randomly around the board.

TITLES:

Stormy Weather Reading
Stormy Day Books
Stormy Reading

BACKGROUND: Navy blue

BORDERS: None

FLOORING: Green burlap

LETTERINGS: Four-inch aluminum foil cutouts (laminate foil before cutting out letters)

PROPS: Large twister tree limb; rain drops; twigs and limbs; small tin house; tornado safety tips; clear hail-like glass balls; books about weather

INSTRUCTIONS: Staple background to walls of the showcase. Build up floor of the showcase with clumps of newspapers and clusters of books. Cover these mounds with green burlap. Make a twister from a tree limb with two large branches. Wrap a package of cotton batting around the limb. Because the limb is one piece and spreads out to two limbs, it makes the essential shape of a twister. Paint the twister with acrylic paint by dabbing black and gray paint over the cotton batting. Stick twigs and limbs into the batting. Place the twister a little left of center in the showcase. Pull down fingers of batting to make the twister look more lifelike. Staple slogan on the right upper side of the showcase. Place books about weather and tornadoes on the mounds in the floor of the showcase. Put tornado safety tips in front of the showcase so that students can easily read them. Place a small house upside down on the hills. Scatter twigs and small limbs around the green burlap. Scatter hail-like glass balls around the showcase.

TITLES:

April Showers Bring Reading Hours
April Showers of Books
Rainy-Day Reading

BACKGROUND: Navy blue and a green strip of grass

BORDERS: None

LETTERINGS: White pin backs or cutouts

PROPS: Umbrella; aluminum foil raindrops; list of books with *April* in the titles

INSTRUCTIONS: Staple background to the showcase. Staple grass strip to the bottom of the board. Attach a partially opened umbrella in the upper right corner of the showcase by thumbtacking it in several places on the inside. Heavy-duty tape was also taped around the umbrella shaft under the top part of the umbrella; then thumbtacked. Put slogan in upper left side of board. Stick raindrops randomly around board with rubber cement. Tape a list of books with *April* in the titles to the umbrella.

TITLES:

Read the Rain Away
Rainy-Day Reading
April Showers Bring Reading Hours

BACKGROUND: Dark blue

BORDERS: None

FLOORING: Artificial green turf

LETTERINGS: White pin backs or cutouts

PROPS: Umbrella; doll in raincoat (if a raincoat is not available, substitute any type of suitable apparel); white fence; aluminum foil raindrops; flowers; tree limb; green leaves; books

INSTRUCTIONS: Staple background to walls of showcase. Place the artificial turf in the floor of the showcase. Place the tree limb on the right side and slanted back to the left. Place green vines or green leaves on the tree limb. Put the white fence on the left side. Add spring flowers behind the fence. Place the slogan in the upper left quadrant. Put a doll under an umbrella under the tree. Add books to the doll's hands and around the floor. Attach a book to the doll's hands. Place other books on weather around the floor. Attach books to the side showcase walls using slings. Use rubber cement to attach raindrops to walls and windows.

TITLES:

Libraries Are the Keys to Your Future
Books Are the Keys to Your Future
Reading Is the Key to Your Future

BACKGROUND: Blue-and-gold patterned wrapping paper

BORDERS: Gold

LETTERINGS: White pin backs

PROPS: Keys (plaster or cutouts)

INSTRUCTIONS: Staple background to the board. Staple or put up slogan, centering it on the board. Perhaps make the word *Keys* larger and out of gold paper. Arrange large keys (purchased or made with aid of the opaque projector) randomly around the slogan.

TITLES:

Books: The Key to Success
Libraries Are the KEYS to Your Future
Reading Is the Key to Your Future

BACKGROUND: Blue-and-gold patterned wrapping paper

BORDERS: Gold

FLOORING: Blue carpet

LETTERINGS: White pin backs or cutouts

PROPS: Gold plaster keys (purchase or make using the overhead projector); white column; list of instructions for guessing contest; plastic clear container for keys; list of rules; keys (hundreds of them); books about education, ACT tests, and SAT tests

INSTRUCTIONS: Staple background to walls of showcase. Staple border at the top of the showcase walls. Place carpet floor in the showcase. Place the slogan in the top one-third of the showcase. Place plaster column in the middle of the showcase. Borrow keys from the local locksmith for NLW (National Library Week) guessing contest. Arrange keys around the walls of the showcase and fill the clear plastic container with them. Staple the list of rules in lower right side of the showcase. Prop the instructions for the guessing contest in lower left side of the showcase. Stand books about education, ACT tests, and SAT tests on floor of showcase. Lay keys in floor of showcase. Include the number of keys on the walls and floor of the showcase in the final count for the winning number.

TITLES:

Pop into the Library
Pop in for the New Books
Pop in for Fantasy Books

BACKGROUND: Yellow

BORDERS: Red or red-and-yellow stripe

LETTERINGS: Red cutouts

PROPS: Sucker pops; tissue paper in green, brown, purple, and red; Styrofoam balls in assorted sizes (could substitute firmly rolled balls of newspaper); bamboo sticks, small dowel rods (could substitute rolled poster boards or anything to make a stick); book titles on strips of white paper

INSTRUCTIONS: Staple background to board. Staple border to edges. Staple slogan as illustrated. Make sucker pops. Take Styrofoam balls or rolled newspaper balls, insert the sticks into the balls. Cover pop with tissue paper. Twist the paper tightly around the ball. Cut jagged edges from the paper. Pin or staple as many suckers as are needed to balance the board and highlight the slogan. Tape strips of white paper with titles of new books to the sucker pops.

TITLES:

Pop into the Library
"Guess How Many Cups of Popcorn"
Pop into the Library for a New Book

BACKGROUND: Red-and-white stripes (wrapping paper works well)

BORDERS: Red

FLOORING: None

LETTERINGS: Red cutouts

PROPS: Giant-sized clear plastic trash bag (try the custodians as a source); popcorn; popcorn bags; rules sign, if doing a contest; ballots

INSTRUCTIONS: Staple background to showcase walls. Attach border. Staple slogan across the top of the back wall. Air-pop the popcorn into the trash bag. Place the bag of popcorn into the showcase before tying the top of the bag; this allows the popcorn room to be moved and molded into the best position in the showcase. Tie the top of the bag. Staple, open popcorn bags to the side walls, and fill with more popcorn. Randomly place ballots around the floor of the showcase.

VARIATIONS: For the contest, add a sign posting rules (one guess a day, deadline, etc.) and a few ballots scattered around. To measure the corn, pop it into a box and measure by a four-cup measure into the large sack. Measure one sack of corn, then multiply how many sacks you use by that many cups of popped corn. Nearest guess, in cups of popped corn, wins. Faculty and staff have separate category. Prizes are gift certificates for a bookstore.

TITLES:

Dive into Reading
Dive into a Good Book
Dive into Summer Reading

BACKGROUND: Fish patterned wrapping paper or solid sea green paper

BORDERS: None

LETTERINGS: Four-inch orange cutouts

PROPS: Swimming fins; snorkel; diving mask; fish; bubbles (from bubble wrap)

INSTRUCTIONS: Staple background to board. Attach the diving mask in the center of the board. Attach the snorkel by it. Place one fin to the left bottom side of board and the other one to the right bottom side of board. Place the word *Dive* in the upper left corner. Put the word *Into* in the upper right corner. Place the word *Reading* at the bottom of the board under the fins. Attach fish (bought or made on the opaque projector) around the board in strategic places. Rubber cement bubbles cut from green bubble wrap on the background. Place bubbles around the mask.

TITLES:

Dive into Reading
Dive into Summertime Reading
Dive into New Books This Summer

BACKGROUND: Fish patterned wrapping paper

BORDERS: None

FLOORING: Brown artificial turf or artificial green turf

LETTERINGS: Four-inch cutouts or pin backs

PROPS: Pillow person (or doll); snorkel; swimming fins; diving mask; bubbles cut out of green bubble wrap; static cling window decals of fish (could substitute colorful pictures from magazines and laminate); ocean cling stickups; waves; rocks; fish; books about sea life; seashells

INSTRUCTIONS: Staple background to walls of showcase. Staple slogan to the back wall. Put flooring in showcase. Add rocks, fish, crabs, and any other sea creatures in the floor. Dress the pillow person or doll in a swimsuit, swimming fins, snorkel, and mask. Put the doll or person in the lower left side of showcase. Put bubbles on walls of the showcase and make them look as if they are coming from the snorkel. Add more bubbles to the glass walls of the door. Put cling decals and waves on the doors of the showcase. May need to use rubber cement to attach to the glass. Arrange books around props in the floor. Hang books from the showcase walls by using a sling. Scatter seashells around the books, props, and floor of the showcase.

TITLES:

Notable Classics
Classic Reading
Books Are Classic

BACKGROUND: White

BORDERS: Black

LETTERINGS: Black four-inch cutouts

PROPS: Large black music notes; small die-cut black music notes; list of classics; definition of a classic

INSTRUCTIONS: Staple background to board. Add border to edges. Place large black notes on all four corners of the board. Center the slogan. Staple the *Definition of a Classic* and the *Suggested Classic Reading List* under the slogan. Scatter small music notes around the board and attach with rubber cement.

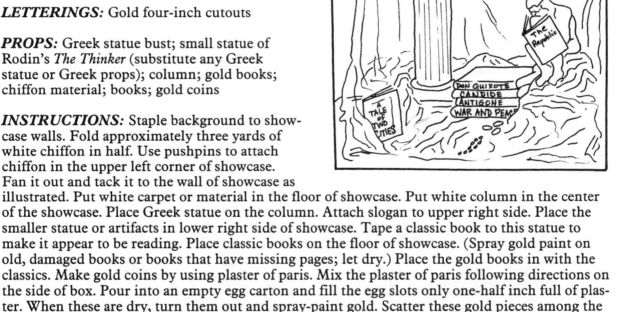

TITLES:

Classic Reading
Books Are a CLASSic ACT
Books Are Classic

BACKGROUND: White

BORDERS: None

FLOORING: White material or white carpet

LETTERINGS: Gold four-inch cutouts

PROPS: Greek statue bust; small statue of Rodin's *The Thinker* (substitute any Greek statue or Greek props); column; gold books; chiffon material; books; gold coins

INSTRUCTIONS: Staple background to show-case walls. Fold approximately three yards of white chiffon in half. Use pushpins to attach chiffon in the upper left corner of showcase. Fan it out and tack it to the wall of showcase as illustrated. Put white carpet or material in the floor of showcase. Put white column in the center of the showcase. Place Greek statue on the column. Attach slogan to upper right side. Place the smaller statue or artifacts in lower right side of showcase. Tape a classic book to this statue to make it appear to be reading. Place classic books on the floor of showcase. (Spray gold paint on old, damaged books or books that have missing pages; let dry.) Place the gold books in with the classics. Make gold coins by using plaster of paris. Mix the plaster of paris following directions on the side of box. Pour into an empty egg carton and fill the egg slots only one-half inch full of plaster. When these are dry, turn them out and spray-paint gold. Scatter these gold pieces among the books and other items. Inexpensive gold pieces may also be found in party stores.

VARIATIONS: Other statues may be used with books propped around them to make them appear to be reading. Use Greek-style vases or more columns. Oval-shaped rocks may also be spray-painted gold to add interest to the showcase.

TITLES:

Rare Books
Rare Reads
Rare Reading

BACKGROUND: Red-and-white checked plastic tablecloth

BORDERS: None

LETTERINGS: Black four-inch cutouts

PROPS: Six paper plates; plastic forks, knives, and spoons; 10 plastic ants; napkins made from red-and-white plastic material or solid white or red material

INSTRUCTIONS: Staple tablecloth to board. Write names of books with food in the titles onto each paper plate. Staple three plates across the bottom of board and staple three across the top of the board exactly across from them as illustrated. Place eating utensil settings as illustrated. Place the napkin under the plastic utensils. Staple slogan in the middle of the board. Staple ants (purchased at a party warehouse store for 15 cents each) to the board, on plates, and across the table.

TITLES:

Rare Books
Rare Reads
Rare Reading Material

BACKGROUND: Blue

BORDERS: None

FLOORING: Green artificial turf and grass strip around base

LETTERINGS: Black four-inch cutouts

PROPS: Small doll picnic table (could substitute a split log) covered with a small red-and-white checked cloth; doll paper plates or small paper plates; doll eating utensils; small charbroiler; books; meat markers that read *rare*; flowers; ants; barbeque tools

INSTRUCTIONS: Staple background to walls of showcase. Staple grass strip around the base. Put green artificial turf on the floor. Place small charbroiler on left side of showcase floor. Staple slogan in the middle of the board. Put a small picnic table on right side of showcase. Hang books and barbeque tools on the showcase walls using slings or pins. Place rare steak markers on the books. Finish scene with flowers, ants, and other outdoor picnic items.

TITLES:

Get Hooked on Reading
Hook a Book
Get Hooked on Books

BACKGROUND: Blue or green wrapping paper printed with fish

BORDERS: Solid or purchased fish border

LETTERINGS: Black pin back

PROPS: Leafy vines; stuffed cloth fish (or paper cutouts); real fish stringer; lures; dowel rod with twine for fishing pole or a real rod and reel; fishing hat; plants; brown paper rocks; other fishy items and equipment; library card

INSTRUCTIONS: Staple the background to the board. Add border to the edges. Put rocks on bottom edge. Staple slogan as illustrated. Drape vines around the edges. Hang fish with titles on the stringer down one side of the board. Position the rod or pole across the board with a fish leaping toward the "bait" of a library card. Arrange greenery across the bottom to resemble a riverbank. Pin hat on the grass.

TITLES:

Get Hooked on Reading
Hook a Book
Get Hooked on Books

BACKGROUND: Fish or fish lure wrapping paper or solid water color

BORDERS: None

FLOORING: Artificial green or brown turf

LETTERINGS: Black pin backs or black cutouts

PROPS: Six stuffed fish or paper cutouts; books about fishing; two fishing hats; fishing rods and poles; log; fish stringer; hooks; lures; artificial plants; leafy vines; Spanish moss

INSTRUCTIONS: Staple the background to the walls of the showcase. Put artificial turf in for the floor. Place the log in the back left and center of the showcase floor. Place leafy vines across the top and sides of the showcase. Put lures and other fishy items in the floor of showcase. Arrange rods and poles in right corner of the showcase. Hang three fish with titles taped on them. Pin the stringer to the right side of the showcase above and in front of the poles and rods. Staple slogan in the top left one-third of the back wall of the showcase. Pin a long fishing line or string to the top of the stringer. Fan it out to the middle of the back wall under the slogan. Attach a giant hook made from poster board, construction paper, or a large real hook. Add a lure below the hook. Pose one of the larger stuffed fish to look as if it is about to strike the hook in the middle of the board as illustrated, or pin the fish on the fishing line. Place books about fishing on the floor of the showcase and propped up in front of the log. Add hooks and lures by the books. Place fishing hats on top of books. Lay two of the fish in the center of the floor of the showcase on the grassy turf. Add Spanish moss to the hanging leafy vines, around the floor of the showcase, and among the books as needed. Insert artificial plants behind and among the books and other props to add balance.

TITLES:

> *Congratulations to the Class of (graduation year)!*
> *Congratulations Graduates*
> *Seniors Have Class*

BACKGROUND: School color

BORDERS: School color

LETTERINGS: Pin back or cutouts in school color or contrasting color

PROPS: Mortar boards and tassels (real or paper cutouts); class roll with spaces beside each name

INSTRUCTIONS: Staple background to the showcase walls. Staple border to edges. Attach slogan across the top. Fasten class roll under the slogan, centered. Arrange mortar boards and tassels around the board. Invite seniors to write their plans for the immediate future (college choice, military, tech school, marriage, work) next to their names.

VARIATIONS: Use rhyming slogans according to the graduation year. (See examples on next page.)

TITLES:

Congratulations to the Class of (graduation year)!
Congratulations Graduates: Seniors Have Class
Seniors Have Class

BACKGROUND: School colors

BORDERS: School color or none

FLOORING: Light material or shredded tissue paper in school colors

LETTERINGS: Pin backs or cutouts in one of the school colors

PROPS: Light-colored material; two pedestals; two busts; two caps and gowns; other graduation accessories according to school (Honor Society collar, tassels); silhouettes of male and female graduates; pin-backed numbers of graduation year

INSTRUCTIONS: Staple background to showcase walls. Place pedestals on each side of the flooring. Drape material around pedestal bases and cover floor. Dress busts in caps and gowns. Fasten silhouettes to side walls. Place busts on the pedestals. Attach slogan to back wall above busts.

VARIATIONS: Scatter "graduation confetti" (tiny foil mortar board cutouts and graduation year numbers) around the bottom of the display. Use rhyming slogans according to the graduation year. Examples: *'08 Is Great, Expect More from '04*, or *Class of '02, We're Proud of You!*

TITLES:

Fan-tastic Books for Summer
Fan-tastic Summer Reading
Fan-tastic Books

BACKGROUND: Light blue (or colors to coordinate with fan designs)

BORDERS: Aqua or darker blue

LETTERINGS: Oriental font printed from computer program and enlarged or pin backs

PROPS: Different sized fans, which may be purchased or constructed; reading list printed in same font as title and include call numbers and authors on the list

INSTRUCTIONS: Staple background to board. Staple border to edges. Staple slogan as illustrated; placing *Fan-tastic* to the left of the fan and *Books for Summer* over the reading list. Staple book list under the slogan as illustrated. Arrange fans around the book list. To make a fan, use patterned paper (plain or with a design)—wallpaper works well. Accordion-pleat a rectangle of paper. Fasten one end with a brad or staple. Open out and pin on board.

TITLES:

Fan-tastic Books for Summer
Fan-tastic Books
Fan-tasy Books

BACKGROUND: Light blue (or colors to coordinate with fan designs)

BORDERS: None

FLOORING: Off-white satin

LETTERINGS: Oriental font from computer program or pin backs

PROPS: Different size fans; electric fan; books; leafy vines; large plant leaves; Oriental fabric

INSTRUCTIONS: Staple background to showcase walls. Arrange off-white satin in floor of showcase. Attach slogan to back walls as illustrated. Staple or use pushpins to attach fans to back wall of showcase. Hang leafy vines down both sides of the showcase. Prop large fan opened in the middle bottom of showcase. Put artificial plant leaves where needed. Stand books up in front of showcase. Place fan around some of the books. Place electric fan in the bottom right of the showcase. Use Oriental fabric draped among books scattered and arranged in stacks. Hang other books with a sling as needed to fill in blank spots in showcase.

TITLES:

Gold Medal Reading
Read for the Gold
Olympic-Style Reading

BACKGROUND: Red, white, and blue flag material

BORDERS: Solid red

LETTERINGS: Red four-inch cutouts

PROPS: Doll wearing gymnastic clothes or exercise clothes; newspaper articles; pictures of winners; magazine covers; books; medal on ribbon

INSTRUCTIONS: Staple background to board. Add border around the edges. Staple slogan to board. Use T-pins and pin the doll to the left side of the board. Attach book with sling as if the doll is balanced upon it. If a doll is not available, add more newspaper articles and coverage. Staple the slogan in place. Staple articles about the Olympics, winners, and medal counts to board. Add books about related subjects. Add the medal on a ribbon under the slogan.

TITLES:

Read for the Gold
Exercise Your Mind
Win with Reading

BACKGROUND: Flag-patterned fabric

BORDERS: None

FLOORING: Wood

LETTERINGS: Red four-inch cutouts

PROPS: Newspaper articles on the Olympics; front page pictures of winners; magazine covers; doll in Olympic clothes; box on which doll is arranged in a gymnastic pose; books; medals; flags

INSTRUCTIONS: Staple background to walls. Staple slogan across the top of the showcase. For Summer Olympics, choose colorful articles and pictures. Arrange these articles attractively. For Winter Olympics (during school time), change the articles daily or if something important happens: It is always interesting to students to keep a medal count. Cover a box with the same fabric as the background. Arrange the doll on the box as if it is performing a gymnastic routine. Add books on various exercise activities across the floor and leaning on the box. Place medals or any other Olympic memorabilia around the exhibit. Add flags if desired.

TITLES:

> *Book an Adventure in Australia*
> *Book a Trip to Australia*
> *Reserve a Trip to Australia*

BACKGROUND: Multipastel wrapping paper

BORDERS: None

LETTERINGS: White pin backs or white four-inch cutouts

PROPS: Tree branch with tropical leaves; Spanish moss; list of books about Australia; koala bears; books about Australia; large artificial plants; leafy vines

INSTRUCTIONS: Staple background to board. Attach slogan to upper part of board. Fasten branch to the left side of the board, thumbtacked or pushpinned twice. Fasten koalas to branch with T-pins, pushpins, or rubber bands. Drape Spanish moss on tree. Staple Spanish moss across the bottom of the showcase. Place book list on right side of board under slogan. Staple leaves randomly to add balance.

TITLES:

Book a Trip to Australia
Book an Adventure to Australia
On the Road Again: Australia
Read All About It: Australia

BACKGROUND: Multipastel fabric or blue paper with clouds

BORDERS: None

FLOORING: Spanish moss

LETTERINGS: White pin backs or white cutouts

PROPS: Tree branch with tropical-style leaves attached; map of Australia; Spanish moss; mom and child stuffed koala bears

INSTRUCTIONS: Staple background to showcase walls. Staple or pin the slogan in upper center of showcase. Put tree limb on the right side of the showcase with the branches going across the left side of showcase. Attach tropical-style leaves from artificial plants to the branches. Place map in lower left corner, partially unfolded. Put more leaves around map. Place the mother and baby koala bears hanging onto the limbs of the tree. Arrange books on Australia around floor of showcase. Place clumps of Spanish moss around books and other items in the showcase until the floor does not show through. Hang leafy vines in the top of showcase. Drape Spanish moss hanging down from vines.

VARIATIONS: Use this showcase format for any country. Change the leaves, tree, animals, maps, and books to highlight the chosen land.

Chapter Four

Lists, Forms, Sources, Suggestions, and Helps

This is the chapter that provides lists, forms, sources, suggestions, and helps. It is hoped that these items will aid the bulletin board and showcase artist in finding and collecting materials to create the boards and showcases featured in this book.

SUPPLY LIST AND SUGGESTED SOURCE

The following lists are suggestions of items that may be used to enhance bulletin boards and showcases. They do not have to be purchased all at once, but start collecting them. The bulletin board and showcase artist may discover alternate ideas and still be able to create the boards and showcases featured in Chapter Three.

Outdoors

twigs and small branches
tree limbs
wood (small logs, stumps)
hay (loose or a large bale)
seashells
rocks (assorted sizes)
leaves

Garage Sales and Home

> newspapers
> keys (start collecting now)
> miniature books
> dolls (assorted sizes and styles)
> carpet scraps (indoor-outdoor and regular)
> boxes (assorted sizes)
> brown paper sacks

School

> opaque projector
> laminator
> letter-cutting machine
> stapler and staples
> thumbtacks
> tape (transparent and masking)

Teacher Supply Store

> borders (assorted colors and design)
> letters (pin back, cutout)

Posters

> travel agencies
> American Library Association
> book fairs

Craft Stores and Discount Stores

Assorted paper types

> craft
> construction
> tissue
> wrapping
> poster board

Party Supplies

> streamers
> balloons
> fans (various sizes and types)

flags (all sizes and countries)
fishnet

Toy Department

garden tools (rake, hoe, shovel)
plastic ducks, insects
dolls on sale

Plants and Leaves

ornamental corn in husks
vines and plants (artificial)
leaves (plastic, paper, fabric, garlands)
Spanish moss

Craft Department

raffia
Styrofoam (cones, circles, sheets, blocks, balls, scraps)
X-ACTO knife
glue gun, glue sticks
pushpins, T-pins, straight pins
cotton batting, stuffing, balls
fabric for background

Home and Garden Supplies

short section of flower-bed trim (white picket fence)
rope, twine, string, fishing line
dowel rods (assorted sizes)
small pedestal or column
trash bags (black, white, pastels)

Holiday Decorations (watch for postseason sales)

small fir tree
snowflakes (plastic and paper)
assorted artificial pumpkins
tree ornaments

MONTH-BY-MONTH SUGGESTIONS

Using a nine-month format allows planning ahead to keep student interest high. High school upperclassmen ask what next month's display will be. Traffic in the hall by the showcase is buzzing when a new showcase is being installed. The students want to guess or suggest what is being featured. Always listen to their comments. The following list suggests events to be featured each month:

AUGUST

Back to School
Biography As History Month
Book Lovers Day (August 9)
National Aviation Day (August 19)
Romance Awareness Month
Nineteenth Amendment Ratified (women can vote!) August 18, 1920
Romance Books

SEPTEMBER

Back to School
Labor Day (first Monday in September)
National Hispanic Heritage Month (September 15–October 15)
Grandparents Day
Citizenship Day
Fall (September 20)
Equinox
Banned-Book Week (last week of September)
American Indian Day (fourth Friday in September)
Fall Sports

OCTOBER

Autumn
Fall
Harvests
National Crime Prevention Month
National Domestic Violence Awareness Month
American Library Association Founded (October 6)
National Children's Day (October 8)
Columbus Day (October 12)

United Nations Day (October 24)
Halloween (October 31)
Mysteries, Horror, and Terror Books

NOVEMBER

Elections
Veterans Day (November 11)
Native American or National Indian Heritage Month
Harvest Time
National Children's Book Week
Thanksgiving (fourth Thursday in November)
Historical Fiction
Basketball Resumes

DECEMBER

World AIDS Day (December 1)
Holiday Season
Solstice
Winter
Hannukah
Christmas
Ramadan (December 20–January 17)
Kwanza (December 26–January 1)
Winter Sports

JANUARY

New Year's Day
Twelfth Night (January 5)
Epiphany (January 6)
Martin Luther King's Birthday
Science Awareness Month
National Book Month
Robert E. Lee born (January 19)
Inauguration Day (January 20)
Chinese New Year and Vietnamese New Year (January–February)

FEBRUARY

American Heart Month
American History Month
Black History Month
National Freedom Day (February 1)
Groundhog Day
St. Valentine's Day (February 14)
Future Homemakers of America Week
Future Farmers of America Week
Romance Books
Winter Olympics (every four years)

MARCH

National History Month
Spring
St. Patrick's Day (March 17)
Spring Sports
Women's Studies
Women's History Month
United Nations Day
International Women's Day
Windy Weather
Kites

APRIL

April Fools' Day (April 1)
National Library Week
Rainy Weather
Stormy Weather
Pan American Day (April 14)
National Poetry Month
Pulitzer Prizes Awarded
National Science and Technology Week
Reading Is Fun Week
Earth Day (April 22)
Shakespeare's Birthday (April 23, 1616)
Baseball Resumes

MAY

May Day (May 1)
National Physical Fitness and Sports Month
Cinco de Mayo
V-E Day in Europe (May 8)
Mother's Day (second Sunday in May)
Graduation Day
Armed Forces Day (third Saturday in May)
Memorial Day (last Monday in May)
National Teachers Day (last Monday in May)

JUNE

World History and Culture
Solstice
Summer Reading
Jefferson Davis' Birthday (June 3)
Flag Day (June 14)
Magna Carta Day (signed June 15, 1215)
Father's Day (third Sunday in June)

JULY

Summer Olympics
Independence Day (July 4)
Hot Reads
Celebrate America
Bastille Day in France (July 14)

MONTH ___October___

YEAR	SHOWCASE	BULLETIN BD #1	BULLETIN BD #2
1994	"Scary Books." Bale of hay, scarecrow, leaves	"Ghost Readers Try the 100's." Ghost buster-type of ghosts	"Spooktacular Media." Kit from Upstart
1995	"Boooks Are Real Treats." Large candy corn, peanut butter kisses, suckers	"Creature Features" poster of werewolf, Dracula, Frankenstein	"Get a life . . . Read." Shar pei poster
1996	"Phantastic Classics." *Phantom of the Opera* memorabilia	"Fall for Books." Leaves, book titles	"Boootiful Books." Ghosts, mysteries
1997	"Spine-Tingling Books." Skeleton reading books under spooky tree	"Wrapped Up in Books." Small skeleton wrapped like a mummy reading	"Notable Books for College-Bound Reading." Music notes
1998	"Sizzling Suspense." Tree, moon, pumpkins, pot of books	"Creature Features." Dracula, Wolfman, Frankenstein, spiders	"Boooks Are Real Treats!" Candy corn, suckers, kisses, mints

MONTH _____

YEAR	SHOWCASE	BULLETIN BD #1	BULLETIN BD #2

YEAR 1997–98

YEAR	SHOWCASE	BULLETIN BD #1	BULLETIN BD #2
AUGUST	"Reading Is Timeless." Big Ben	Garfield posters, letters "We're Back!!!"	Mel Gibson; ALA "Read" Poster (which is great hit with faculty)
SEPTEMBER	"Get a Kick Out of Reading." Pillow person, soccer	"Kick Off the Year to a Good Start with Reading." Shoe and leg	"What are you cut out to be??" paper dolls
OCTOBER	"Sizzling Suspense." Tree, moon, pumpkins, pot of books	"Creature Features." Dracula, Wolfman, Frankenstein	"Boooks Are Real Treats." Candy corn, suckers, peppermints
NOVEMBER	"Give Thanks for Books." Critters read around log and stumps	"Rake in a Good Book." Rake and leaves, basket	"Tree-mendous Fall Reading." Tree, leaves
DECEMBER	"Present the Joy of Reading." Santa reads to animals	"Give the Gift of Reading." Reindeer head, present	"Wrapped Up in Reading." Packages, ribbons
JANUARY	"Winterize with Reading." Auto info snow scene, dolls	"Read in the New Year." Polar bear and party hats, etc.	"Snow Time Is Book Time." Snowman
FEBRUARY	"Read to Your Sweetheart." Gorillas and monkeys	"Sweet Heart Reading." Valentine candy box	"Devoted Dog Tales." Fake fur, Scottie
MARCH	"Swing into Spring Reading." Bats, golf clubs, racquets	"Debug Your Brain: Read!" Ladybugs	"Big Hits." Baseballs and players, Styrofoam balls
APRIL	"Stormy Weather Reading." Tornado, raindrops, safety tips	"April Showers Bring Reading Hours." Umbrella	"Libraries Are the Keys to Your Future." Keys
MAY	"Get Hooked on Reading." Stuffed fish, lures, etc.	"Congratulations Graduates." Mortar boards, grad year	"Rare Books." Paper plates, red-and-white-checked tablecloth
JUNE	"Fan-tastic Books for Summer." Fans' lists of books	"Cool Cats Read." Rock-and-roll cat, puppet	"Stay Cool This Summer: Read!" Pillow person, sand
JULY	"Gold Medal Reading." Feature Olympics	"Book an Adventure in Australia." Koala bears	"Hot Reading." Stove, pots and pans

YEAR _____

YEAR	SHOWCASE	BULLETIN BD #1	BULLETIN BD #2
AUGUST			
SEPTEMBER			
OCTOBER			
NOVEMBER			
DECEMBER			
JANUARY			
FEBRUARY			
MARCH			
APRIL			
MAY			
JUNE			
JULY			

BIBLIOGRAPHY

Microsoft Encarta '95 Electronic Encyclopedia, 1995 edition, CD-ROM.

SOURCES FOR IDEAS AND SUPPLIES

ALA Graphics
American Library Association
50 E. Huron Street
Chicago, IL 60611

Demco
PO Box 7488
Madison, WI 53707-7488

GoneReadin@aol.com

Upstart
W5527 Highway 106
PO Box 800
Fort Atkinson, WI 53538-0800

Index

A "B" after the page number indicates Bulletin Boards; a "S" indicates Showcases.

FROM LIBRARIES UNLIMITED

LET'S CELEBRATE TODAY: Calendars, Events, and Holidays
Diana F. Marks

Following a calendar format, this book lists historic events, literary achievements, famous firsts, inventions, birthdays, holidays from around the world, and more. At least three entry-related learning activities are given for each day. Use it as a daily activity guide, rainy day resource, or an idea source for the bulletin board. **Grades K–12.**
xvi, 337p. 8½x11 paper ISBN 1-56308-558-5

THE BOOKMARK BOOK
Carolyn S. Brodie, Debra Goodrich, and Paula K. Montgomery

Delight students, encourage learning, and build library research skills with these 280 handsome, reproducible bookmarks. They cover topics from art (e.g., finger puppet patterns) and music (e.g., biographies of composers) to math (e.g., metric chart), science (e.g., insect identification), social studies (e.g., members of the U.S. Supreme Court), and on and on. Each bookmark includes a question or instructions to motivate students to read more or to search for further information. **All Levels.**
viii, 100p. 8½x11 paper ISBN 1-56308-300-0

BOOKS, BOOKS, BOOKS: A Treasury of Clip Art
Darcie Clark Frohardt

This beautiful collection of copyright-free clip art—all on the subject of books—can be used in producing flyers, posters, newsletters, bulletin boards, bookmarks, and dozens of other forms of visual communication. Chapters cover seven subject areas: Just Books, People with Books, Animals, Nursery Rhyme and Storybook Characters, Holidays, Sports and Activities, and Borders.
vi, 104p. 8½x11 paper ISBN 1-56308-265-9

NEWBERY AND CALDECOTT TRIVIA AND MORE FOR EVERY DAY OF THE YEAR
Claudette Hegel

Pique student interest in reading with more than 1,000 fascinating facts and tantalizing tidbits of information on award-winning and classic books, authors, and illustrators. Arranged in calendar format, many of the facts correspond with a birthday or book publication anniversary. Great for newsletters, bulletin boards, or introducing lessons in author studies. **All Levels.**
xiii, 167p. 8½x11 paper ISBN 1-56308-830-4

100 LIBRARY LIFESAVERS: A Survival Guide for School Library Media Specialists
Pamela S. Bacon

Ever feel like you're drowning in an overwhelming number of tasks? These ready-to-use lifesavers will help you stay afloat while you successfully manage your facilities. You'll find advice on subjects ranging from completing library inventory, handling overdue materials, and starting a book club to teaching Internet research skills and improving public relations.
xxi, 317p. 8½x11 paper ISBN 1-56308-750-2

For a free catalog or to place an order, please contact Libraries Unlimited.
•Phone: 800-237-6124 • Fax: 303-220-8843 • Visit: www.lu.com
•Mail to: Dept. B043 • P.O. Box 6633 • Englewood, CO 80155-6633